At Issue

| Bulimia

Other Books in the At Issue Series:

At Issue

| Bulimia

Adriane Ruggiero, Book Editor

GREENHAVEN PRESS

An imprint of Thomson Gale, a part of The Thomson Corporation

Detroit • New York • San Francisco • New Haven, Conn. • Waterville, Maine • London

THOMSON

GALE

Christine Nasso, *Publisher*
Elizabeth Des Chenes, *Managing Editor*

© 2008 The Gale Group.

Star logo is a trademark and Gale and Greenhaven Press are registered trademarks used herein under license.

For more information, contact:
Greenhaven Press
27500 Drake Rd.
Farmington Hills, MI 48331-3535
Or you can visit our Internet site at http://www.gale.com

LIBRARY OF CONGRESS CATALOGING-IN-PUBLICATION DATA

Bulimia / Adriane Ruggiero, book editor.
  p. cm. -- (At issue)
  Includes bibliographical references and index.
  ISBN-13: 978-0-7377-3673-1 (hardcover)
  ISBN-13: 978-0-7377-3674-8 (pbk.)
  1. Bulimia--Juvenile literature. 2. Eating disorders--Juvenile literature.
  I. Ruggiero, Adriane
  RC552.B84B8412 2008
  616.85'263--dc22
                                                            2007028828

ISBN-10: 0-7377-3673-9 (hardcover)
ISBN-10: 0-7377-3674-7 (pbk.)

Printed in the United States of America
10 9 8 7 6 5 4 3 2 1

Contents

Introduction

Most past and current information about eating disorders in the United States has focused on anorexia, bulimia, and binge eating among women and girls. In fact, the image of the anorexic girl or woman has become a stereotype of the person with an eating disorder. This image is beginning to change as more researchers study eating disorders among men and boys. Like girls, boys in our culture seeking social acceptance are being pressured to conform to perceived notions about what constitutes a "good" physical appearance. Unlike girls and women, males with eating disorders are less likely to be identified as having an eating disorder. Males are also less likely to admit to having a problem or to seek help; however, their health problems—both mental and physical—are just as real and dangerous.

In a 2006 study of nearly three thousand American adults conducted by Harvard University Medical School, researchers found that 25 percent of adults with anorexia and bulimia were men and 40 percent with a binge-eating problem were men. These men comprise a large, silent population of sufferers, psychologists say. Those medical professionals treating men with eating disorders pinpoint some of the same issues that drive women to engage in disordered eating behavior: obsession with body image, a strong drive for perfectionism, compulsiveness, and feelings of depression and low-self esteem. Other issues also enter the discussion with regard to men and eating disorders. Some male professional and amateur athletes feel they must control their weight in order to stay competitive. They use starvation and purging as part of a negative and unhealthly fitness regimen. This may apply particularly to sports such as swimming, diving, gymnastics, or wrestling, which require a weigh-in to compete. Some men in professions in which physical appearance is equated with earning power and job success might practice self-starvation or purging in order to retain a marketable appearance of youth, vigor, and sex appeal. This is particularly true for some male actors, dancers, and print and runway models whose slender and boyish looks keep them in demand as bankable commodities. Soldiers fit this profile, too. The military requirements for physical fitness are strict and those who fail to meet the requirements will not win promotion and may be penalized. Researchers also found that men who were overweight as children and teens and who were bullied or teased because of their weight often developed eating disorders.

What makes men reluctant to seek help in dealing with their eating disorders? One of the obstacles has to do with being embarrassed about having a "woman's" problem. If a guy admits to having an eating disorder, then he is seen to be unmanly or homosexual, psychologists say. Men who do seek help in dealing with their anorexia, bulimia, or binge eating often find the medical establishment unprepared to deal with their specific thought processes and experiences. Therapists and recovery centers are generally trained to treat and talk with women about their eating disorder issues. Even the language used in screening tests ("Are you concerned about your hips or the size of your thighs?") is gender-biased. Few men would take such questions seriously or feel comfortable in a rehabilitative environment where they were the sole male or in the minority. In addition, there are just a handful of eating disorder clinics in the United States that have specific programs for men. Some clinics don't even accept male patients. In brief, men are greatly underdiagnosed and underserved when it comes to eating disorders.

What can parents and schools do to help boys and young men avoid disordered eating? All experts agree that getting the anorexic or bulimic child or teen immediate help is the most important action a parent can take. Doctors may not be as perceptive when it comes to diagnosing a young man's eating disorder, therefore parents are under increased pressure to be vigilant with regard to their child's eating habits. School coaches have a special responsibility to their young male athletes to present the issue of eating disorders, discuss it, and monitor the exercise and eating habits of those in their charge. Boys, in general, need to be made more aware of the long-term risks of disordered eating. Convincing all young men and women to overcome the powerful messages our media-driven culture gives out about body image and concepts of beauty is not an easy task.

Recovery programs also need to be customized for male patients. Some experts feel that men in recovery do best when they have their own group and body-image sessions. These provide them with a comfortable place to discuss issues that are relevant to them. They may also need more time in overcoming reluctance to discuss their problems and examining the emotional triggers behind them. Discussing physical problems such as loss of testosterone (as a result of malnourishment) is also easier in an all-male setting. Whatever it takes, boys and men should not feel isolated in their disease.

1

Bulimia: An Overview

Deborah Marcontell Michel and Susan G. Willard

Deborah Marcontell Michel is a clinical assistant professor in the department of psychiatry and neurology at the Tulane University School of Medicine. Susan G. Willard is the director of the Eating Disorders Treatment Center at River Oaks Hospital and is professor in the department of psychiatry and neurology and the department of pediatrics at the Tulane University School of Medicine.

Bulimia is an eating disorder that is psychologically based and involves overeating and then purging to avoid weight gain. The purging is achieved by vomiting, ingesting laxatives or diuretics, or with enemas. Bulimics often exercise obsessively to burn the calories acquired through binge eating. The disease affects 5 to 10 million girls and women and 1 million boys and men. More than 90 percent of bulimics are females and are characterized as chronic dieters who are obsessed with image and control. Their phobias about food are often a way of dealing with serious emotional issues. Bulimia nervosa is a major health concern in the United States and Western societies whose cultures associate thinness with youth, success, and control. These values, along with the desire to have it all—beauty, career, romance—are pressures that can lead to anxiety and fear, which drive women to choose dieting as a solution. Bulimics can get well and stay well with professional counseling and the support of family and friends.

A lthough the formal diagnostic name for this illness is bulimia nervosa, it is better known by the public as bulimia. The disorder is characterized by binge eating, followed by eliminating the calories consumed in compensation for the binge. The bulimic usually either self-induces vomiting or takes laxatives or diuretics in an effort to eliminate the calories. She may diet strictly or fast between eating episodes to undo the damage, or she may exercise excessively in order to prevent weight gain. When binge eating, she feels out of control and believes she cannot stop. To meet the criteria for formal diagnosis, her binges occur at least twice a week over a three-month period, and she is persistently overconcerned with her body size, shape, and weight. This focus on the body strongly influences her negative self-image.

Food Used as a Drug

In spite of repeated binge eating, bulimics often manage to stay within five to ten pounds of normal weight. The typical bulimic is a professional dieter who often gains back the weight she loses and repeatedly feels like a failure. Her interest in her body and dieting becomes an obsession and she will often swing between strict dieting and periods of overeating. At some point in the process, she starts to feel great anxiety and may experience something akin to a "high" by ingesting large amounts of food. Like a drug, the food becomes a calming or numbing substance when anxiety and painful feelings about herself mount. Because of her overconcern with her body and her strong desire to be thin, the bulimic feels that she must get rid of the food and perhaps punish herself for what she considers to have been "bad" behavior. In an attempt to accomplish this task, she turns to purging or excessive exercise, usually within thirty minutes to an hour after the binge. Vomiting is typically induced by putting her fingers down her throat, although some individuals utilize foreign objects (spoons, forks, toothbrushes). These objects can be dangerous in and of themselves. Those who abuse laxatives usually take an excessive number to induce severe diarrhea after a binge and may increase the dosage over time.

As in anorexia, personality changes and emotional conditions are associated with bulimia. Depression is very common. Some of the depressive symptoms are directly related to binge/ purge behaviors, along with the shame, guilt, and embarrassment associated with these practices. Much of the time, though, the depression that occurs is separate from bulimic behavior and has more to do with how the bulimic feels about herself, her family, and her life in general. Anxiety, almost always present, has been shown to play a major role in maintenance of the binge-purge cycle. The soothing and self-nurturing feelings that initially accompany the binge are quickly replaced by extreme concern over the calories consumed and fear of weight gain. In turn, the behaviors that are used to get rid of the calories reduce this anxiety and the cycle continues.

As with anorexics, anxiety disorders in bulimics are often present before the eating disorder develops. As the illness continues, those closest to the bulimic may notice her increased withdrawal and isolation from others, as well as her negative feelings about herself. She may never eat around others for fear of losing control or of being discovered. Greater difficulty with impulse control may be evident; some bulimics engage in stealing, risky sexual behavior, and drug or alcohol abuse. This acting-out may perpetuate a cycle of low self-esteem, depression, and self-destructive behavior, which creates further personality changes that are often of a rebellious nature.

Secret Ritual

People who have these periodic binges followed by purging, fasting, and/or exercise are aware that their relationship with food is abnormal and out of control. At first the behaviors to get rid of the calories may feel like the perfect answer to a dieter's dilemma. As the food intake increases and control is lost, however, bulimia becomes a nightmare for its victims. They are usually quite private and ritualistic because of the secretive and remorseful nature of the disorder. Even though the physical problems associated with the disease may become severe, the bulimic may still be reluctant to tell her physician what she is doing to her body. A great number of individuals are burdened with the illness for many years before telling a single person.

When friends and/or family become aware of the binge-eating and purging, it is usually because they notice large amounts of food missing or recognize signs of purging in the bathroom. When first confronted, most bulimics deny the problem. They often become angry or hostile and may feel intruded upon when someone dares to enter their secret world. Yet somewhere inside, they may wish to be discovered so that something can be done to stop the despised and seemingly never-ending cycle.

It is not unusual for the bulimic's dentist to be the first to suspect her illness.

As the illness progresses, binge-eating episodes become more frequent and the amount of food consumed during a binge increases. Relationships, work, school performance, and self-esteem often suffer dramatically. The depression associated with bulimia can be severe; unfortunately, suicide is sometimes viewed as the only solution. It is imperative that bulimics receive prompt professional attention once the disorder is discovered.

Problems Caused by Bulimia

In normal-weight bulimics, most of the medical complications of starvation seen in anorexics are not present. However, the same serious problems related to purging . . . described in individuals with anorexia (the loss of important body fluids and minerals) occur in persons with bulimia. We do not know what percentage of bulimics die from complications of the illness, but we do know that many deaths have been reported and that most bulimics have an assortment of medical problems associated with the disease.

Dental Problems Are Common

Common complications, though certainly not the most serious, are dental and throat problems. It is not unusual for the bulimic's dentist to be the first to suspect her illness. Cavities, enamel erosion, persistent throat irritation, and chronic hoarseness can be the result of frequent vomiting. Abdominal pain, heartburn, and/or stomach cramps are frequent complaints, usually associated with overeating or purging behavior. Often bulimics will have swollen glands at the angle of the jaw, a result of bingeing and purging. Swelling or bloating over the stomach or abdominal area and in the extremities (fingers and toes) is caused by the fluid imbalance created by purging. Frequent menstrual irregularities are also seen, and sometimes bulimics lose their cycles altogether. The menstrual problems are usually due to excessive exercise and/or low body fat content. Dehydration, dryness of the skin, or a fine rash can result when too much body fluid is eliminated. Sometimes calluses or scars occur over the knuckles of the hand used to purge, from chronic abrasion by the teeth when the fingers are forced down the throat repeatedly to induce vomiting. The most serious, life-threatening consequences of bulimia are esophageal tears, stomach rupture, kidney failure, heart failure, and cardiac arrest.

Not much is known about the course of untreated bulimia. According to clinic samples, however, disturbed eating is likely to persist for at least several years. Some individuals may have periods of spontaneous improvement and then relapse. Others follow a more chronic course, in which the symptoms worsen over time. Community samples have reported modest levels of spontaneous improvement.

All Eating Disorders Must Be Taken Seriously

When an individual presents with symptoms of an eating disorder but does not have all the specific symptoms of either anorexia or bulimia, a diagnosis of "Eating Disorder Not Otherwise Specified" is made. Common examples include someone who has all the symptoms of anorexia nervosa but is not yet 15 percent below normal body weight or who has not yet missed her period for three consecutive cycles, or a person who does not binge and/or purge as often as stipulated to meet the psychiatric definition of bulimia nervosa.

Even though these individuals do not meet the formal diagnostic criteria, their disorders must be taken seriously. The psychological changes and disturbances associated with anorexia or bulimia are likely to be present in one form or another. In addition, the medical complications seen in anorexia and bulimia apply to these persons, depending on which symptoms are present. For example, someone who has not yet dropped 15 percent below normal weight but has quickly lost weight may suffer from medical problems associated with rapid weight loss. Finally, it is likely that an individual with these symptoms will progress into more severe eating disordered behavior if prompt professional intervention is not sought. Much of the information presented regarding the development and treatment of anorexia and bulimia applies to those with an unspecified eating disorder. The issues involved in the development of the eating disorders are similar, whereas treatment will vary depending on the type of eating disordered behavior involved.

2

Many Bulimics Appear Healthy

B. Timothy Walsh and V.L. Cameron

B. Timothy Walsh is the Ruane Professor of Pediatric Psychopharmacology in the College of Physicians and Surgeons at Columbia University and founder of the Eating Disorders Research Unit at the New York State Psychiatric Institute. V.L. Cameron is a writer based in New York City.

Recognizing an eating disorder such as bulimia in a child is often difficult for many parents. Parents may point to a child's finicky eating habits as the reason for weight loss. Or shame may prompt parents to deny the fact that their daughter or son is actually purging food in order to maintain an ideal body image. Or they may think that their child has another disease that accounts for the changes in weight. The disappearance of food and signs of vomiting on clothing or in the bathroom are telltale signs of bulimia and often reveal the bulimic's secret to their parents. But many parents warn that the illness is among the most difficult to detect on account of the healthy appearance many bulimics convey. The best way to learn the truth about the disease in the child or adult bulimic is to listen to the individual and observe their behavior.

"Food was always a big part of Linda's life," Kay says of her daughter, who was diagnosed with bulimia nervosa. "Even when she was in kindergarten, she would take a box of cereal or crackers, go sit in front of the TV, and eat out of the box. She was also larger and more developed than most kids her age. As time went on, she became self-conscious about her size."

A month before Linda turned 12, she got the stomach flu, was out of school for a week, and lost ten pounds.

Losing Weight Got Linda Noticed

"When Linda returned to school," Kay says, "she got so much attention for losing weight that she decided to lose more. Eventually, she stopped eating anything but oranges. We kept trying to get her to eat, but nothing worked, and after four months, she'd lost 50 pounds. Then she suddenly started eating again. We were thrilled, but we were also amazed because she wasn't gaining any weight." She also began spending more and more time in the bathroom and, when Kay would go in to clean up, it appeared as if someone had vomited. Kay noticed changes in Linda's moods, too.

"Suddenly she wasn't our sweet little girl anymore. She started having trouble getting along with her sisters and grandmother, plus we also noticed lots of food disappearing. I would get home from the store and swear I had bought bagels, but the next morning when I went to look for them, they would be gone. I asked everybody in the house where they were and they all claimed they hadn't seen them. I started questioning whether the bagels had even made it home from the grocery store or if I had accidentally left them in the basket or on the counter."

According to Kay, Linda was also not the neatest person in the world and arguments ensued about her room always being a mess. An agreement was finally struck that if Linda wanted to leave it that way, she'd have to keep her bedroom door closed and would be responsible for putting away her clothes after they were laundered. After Linda left for camp the following summer, Kay went into Linda's room to give it a thorough cleaning.

[I]t is only when a binge is over that the person experiences feelings of disgust and shame, which they may then try to assuage with the comforting effect of another binge.

"I found all these clothes that she'd purged in. They were shoved into drawers, under the bed, and stuffed in her soccer bag. There were enough clothes to fill a large lawn-size garbage bag. How there wasn't an incredible stench in that room is still beyond me. And a lot of the purging was dark matter, which I later found out from professionals was bile because that was how hard she was purging."

Linda exhibited classic symptoms of bulimia nervosa, a disease that was first clearly recognized as a disorder by the psychiatric community in 1979. It is characterized by episodes of binge eating large quantities of food during a short period of time, followed by purging (most commonly via self- or drug-induced vomiting, but laxatives and diuretics are also used), restricting food intake (via fasting or extreme dieting), or exercising excessively—all in an effort to avoid gaining weight from the binges. When vomiting is used, such binges can be repeated over several hours—the binger eats, vomits, and then eats again, with some patients reporting that they binge and purge up to 20 times during a 24-hour period.

Many Cannot Remember Bingeing

While the binge-purge cycle of behavior is almost always done in secret and accompanied by feelings of self-disgust, shame, and being out of control, some claim they actually have no memory of binge eating and don't really taste the food they consume. Instead, the binge provides a sedative effect, almost as if the food they're eating acts like a tranquilizing drug that helps them calm down and relieve stress. In such cases, it is only when the binge is over that the person experiences feelings of disgust and shame, which they may then try to assuage with the comforting effect of another binge.

The obsessive concern with shape and weight that characterizes anorexia nervosa is also a prominent feature of bulimia nervosa. The following story from Toni, now an adult recovering from bulimia nervosa, illustrates the extent to which such concerns drove her when she was a teen:

"I'd always been somewhat obsessed with how much I weighed, but never got to the point of starving myself because I loved food too much and couldn't give it up," Toni says. "I pretty much weighed the same thing my whole life, but had to work hard not to gain weight. Each day I'd decide what to eat and, if I had lunch, I either wouldn't eat dinner or, if I did, I'd eat something light, like a salad with no dressing or a small apple." One day, however, Toni forgot she'd been invited to a friend's house for dinner and went ahead and ate what she considered a "huge" lunch (in this case, a burger and fries). Upon returning home at the end of the day, she remembered the dinner invitation and became extremely distressed.

Planning to Purge

"I thought about what a good cook my friend's mom was and realized there would undoubtedly be lots of irresistible food I couldn't possibly pass up," Toni says. "Thinking I couldn't eat two big meals in one day, I suddenly got what I considered a brilliant idea: what goes in always comes out, so why not merely help it along?"

That was the day Toni decided to make herself vomit. She found it surprisingly easy to do and afterwards was absolutely euphoric because she felt cleansed and fresh and ready to partake of whatever delicious food her friend's mother might serve. However, the evening became a blur because she kept thinking of herself as "gobbling up everything in sight."

"While I was eating, it was like I was in a trance and later imagined that it was probably a disgusting spectacle," she says. In hindsight, she now realizes that she really didn't eat much more than anyone else at the table. "Truth be told, I probably ate less than anyone there, but I still hated myself for 'pigging out' and, as soon as I returned home, I made myself throw up again." Thus began a pattern of eating and then purging that would continue for years until Toni finally sought treatment at the behest of her boyfriend (later to become her husband). Yet to this day, she still has issues revolving around food and battles the urge to purge every time she eats more than she thinks she should.

"I still get a little panicked when I'm invited to a party, especially if the host or hostess tells me about all the great food they're going to serve. I guess that's the greatest irony of being bulimic. Because I've basically maintained the same weight over the years, no one ever suspects I have an eating disorder, so they continue to natter on about food without realizing how much it can torment me."

Toni's story also illustrates the point that, unlike those with anorexia nervosa—when self-starvation eventually gives them away physically, no matter how hard they try to hide it—people with bulimia nervosa stay close to or within their normal weight range and can appear perfectly healthy. As one parent says, "In most cases, you can't tell if someone has bulimia just by looking at them. You really have to listen to them and pay attention to their behavior." Indeed, bulimia nervosa is often so hard to spot that it can go undetected for years.

3

Bulimics Are Driven by an Idea of a "Good" Body

Sharlene Hesse-Biber

Sharlene Hesse-Biber is a professor of sociology at Boston College and Director of the Women's Studies Program. She is the author, coauthor, or coeditor of several books, including Am I Thin Enough Yet? *and* Working Women in America.

Most American women want to be thin and many are willing to go to extremes to achieve their goal, even if it includes engaging in disordered eating. American culture propagandizes the idea of the thin woman being a valued woman, and families, schools, and the media affirm it by praising those who conform to the ideal. The net result is that girls and women are led to sacrifice their bodies and health to the cult-like pursuit of an ultrathin ideal. Those who are involved in the cult of thinness have a shared sense of sacrifice in their worship of thinness and its equation with beauty and happiness.

. . . If you're wise, exercise all the fat off.
Take it off over here, over there.
When you're seen anywhere with your hat off,
Wear a marcelled wave in your hair.
Take care of all those charms,
And you'll always be in someone's arms.
Keep young and beautiful,
If you want to be loved.

Sharlene Hesse-Biber, *The Cult of Thinness*. Danvers, MA: Oxford University Press, 2007, pp. 152–153, 155–157, 159–164, 169–175. Copyright © 2007 by Oxford University Press, Inc. Republished with permission of Oxford University Press.

The words of a popular song echo a powerful message in our culture—that only the beautiful and thin are valued and loved. Reiterated by families, peers, and the school environment, this notion is taken seriously by many young women. So seriously, in fact, that anorexia nervosa (starvation dieting, severe weight loss, obsession with food) and bulimia (compulsive binge eating, followed by purging through self-induced vomiting or laxatives) occur 10 times more frequently in women than in men. These syndromes usually develop during adolescence and, until recently, were more prevalent among upper-and middle-class women. . . .

Culture Expects Thinness

Disorderly eating and obsession with food is a widely accepted way to deal with weight and body image issues in a culture where thinness "symbolizes beauty, attractiveness, fashionability, health, achievement, and control." *It is normative behavior for women who are part of the Cult of Thinness*, those who are socialized to apologize for their appetites. Best-selling author and therapist Kim Chernin adds, "Women today, because they cannot bring their natural body into culture without shame and apology, are driven to attack and destroy that body. . . . Women today seem to be practicing genocide against themselves, waging a violent war against the female body precisely because there are no indications that the female body has been invited to enter culture." Commenting on our cultural fear of fat, a leading eating disorders therapist, Nancy J. Kolodny, writes, "The flip side of glorifying thinness is degrading fat, which results in a cultural phenomenon called 'weight prejudice.' . . . Over 50% of females ages 18–25 'would prefer to be run over by a truck than be fat,' and two-thirds of those surveyed 'would rather be mean or stupid' than fat!"

Strategies for weight reduction have unintended consequences. Dieters know severe food restriction over time may trigger an uncontrollable binge. Women who tamper with their body's natural metabolism through dieting, bingeing, and purging may find they gain weight on fewer calories. Excessive exercise can lead to injury or burnout, or even halt menstruation. All of this fosters constant weight and body image preoccupation and may lead to depression and in its wake serve to push women toward the eating disordered end of the continuum, resulting in full-blown eating disorders with their accompanying psychopathologies.

Some of the young women I talked with demonstrated anorectic and bulimic behavior—they engaged in calorie restriction, chronic dieting, bingeing and purging, diuretics or laxatives, or extreme exercise to control their weight. However, they did *not* exhibit the full constellation of psychological traits usually associated with an eating disorder, such as maturity fears, interpersonal distrust, and perfectionism. Some researchers refer to this pattern as "imitative anorexia," "subclinical eating disorders," or "weight preoccupation." I refer to it as *culturally induced* eating—a pattern of eating-disordered symptoms in otherwise psychologically "normal" women.

Colleges and universities across the country are reporting dramatic increases in eating disorders

---

This group of women appears to be driven in large part by the social and economic rewards of looking "right" and "good," notions driven by capitalism and patriarchal systems of profit and control. They are the primary motivators of a culturally induced eating disorder. This is not to say that placing extreme pressures on the body will not disrupt their physiological or psychological well-being, or that manipulating food intake cannot assuage psychological stress or trauma after the disorder develops. But if psychological struggles have not driven the individual to clinical manifestation of anorexia or bulimia, then there are different agents at work.

The college women and young girls who shared their stories with me reside along a "continuum" of eating and body image disturbance. At the one end are those few young women I interviewed who exhibit minimal distress in dealing with their food intake, weight, and body image. At the other end of this scale reside those who struggle mightily with these issues and in fact manifest full-blown clinical eating disorders; this group is also small. It turned out that the vast majority of college age women and young girls I talked with lie in between the two poles of this continuum—that part I call "The Cult of Thinness." During their college careers and postcollege years, some women may move up and down this continuum, while others remain at the more eating-disordered end. . . .

Middle Group Is Much Ignored

Much of the self-help literature on eating disorders and treatment protocols ignores this large middle group, and there remains a lack of understanding of the role that the environment—especially the micro and macro environment of women's lives—plays in the genesis of their position along the "Cult of Thinness" continuum. It is these micro environmental factors that we take up in this [viewpoint]—those factors in our immediate family, peer group, and school environment—that often echo the wider societal cultural pressures on women to "be a slender body." . . .

The majority of women in my sample used disorderly eating primarily for socially correct thinness. I interviewed Suzanna a year after she graduated from college. She traced the beginnings of her body image problems to her junior year, when she and two roommates effectively joined the Cult of Thinness:

> For the first 2 years of college there was really no problem. Eating was sort of the thing, "Let's go to dinner with these people" and "I'll meet you for lunch" and so on. In fact, I maintained my three meals a day routine.
>
> Then things changed drastically.

I always had a good self-image until I roomed with a group of girls who are my closest friends, and super weight conscious. Now that I can look back on it I really can see how out of whack it was. They sort of became my family and . . . their weight was the thing. . . . One of them looked very skinny to me. She was like 5'8" and had a beautiful shape, very thin. She did not eat—I think she lived on cigarettes and soda. She was really bad. There were days, there were weeks where she wouldn't eat solid food. Her cousin, another roommate, also had very strange eating patterns. She was a little overweight because she would eat in hiding. She would try to be like her cousin all day long and not eat. But you'd always hear her eating something in the middle of the night. . . . Junior and senior year I really went crazy living with them. I would go on diets with them . . . liquid diets for days. I remember. I was in the library and I felt dizzy. They both made me feel very heavy. To this day, I'll never be skinny enough. Whenever I saw them they would say "you have 5 or 10 to go." And it bothers me because I'm so used to their mind-set. . . . The weeks I wouldn't eat they would remark, "Oh, Suzanna you are doing great and you look good." And they were so happy because I guess the more the merrier.

I would return home during college breaks, eating just oranges and Diet Coke. And my parent's didn't like that at all. They were paying all this money for a food plan and they would say "go eat" and "don't skip meals." So back there my logical sense would come through—then I'd be on campus and I'd decide I needed lunch and I would go eat by myself. And I'd feel very good about it. And I just wouldn't tell my roommates because they really had problems with it. . . . There were times I would get mad at them. During my senior year we had an apartment. I would have a really good time cooking for myself and my other roommates. And the cousins would pick at it and that would get me very angry, I guess they did that because they felt they weren't really eating.

I did have a third roommate named Sonia, who would be the only one to occasionally eat with me. Sounds so horrible. But she had a stronger personality than I did because she would tell these two cousins to their face that they were crazy! And I would just try to be the middle person and respect how they felt and say okay.

After I left school it took me awhile to get back into my old eating patterns. Now I think I'm eating just as normally as I did in high school. Working every day and I really need my breakfast, lunch, and supper. I'll go through my times and try to cut down a little bit but it's definitely healthier. College was a different swing.

Suzanna's Thinness Obsession Is Brief

The disordered eating Suzanna fell into, influenced by her roommates' values, is distinctly different from an eating disorder. She avoided the slippery slope of thinness-at-any-cost obsession, and once she left that social environment she returned to "normal" eating. Suzanna was lucky her Cult of Thinness membership was only brief. Others are not so fortunate.

Children learn who they are by studying the adults around them, and the family is a child's first interpreter of the larger world. Some families repeat the cultural values of thinness, while others modify the message. Women raised in families who are hypercritical of their daughters' weight place them at greater risk of experiencing disordered eating patterns. Furthermore, teasing about weight and body image during early childhood can lead to a detrimental impact on young girls' body images in later life. Barbara's case is an extreme example of how parents amplify the message that to be beautiful is to be loved. This message dominated her life, fostering a full-blown eating disorder.

Barbara was 20 when I interviewed her . . . . She appeared to be a happy, average-weight, well-adjusted college coed, but

I had had a 2-year ongoing dialogue with her about weight, body image, and her chronic anorexia and bulimia. Her hidden history of anorexia started in seventh grade; her bulimia began in the ninth grade and continued throughout high school and college.

Barbara's Father Has High Standards of Beauty

Barbara's parents had serious marital problems. Her father, toward whom she felt a great deal of ambivalence, had very high standards of feminine beauty. Her own sense of femininity developed as she observed how difficult it was for her mother to live up to her father's expectations. Clinical psychologist Margo Maine writes, "A girl develops beliefs about feminine behavior by watching her father interact with women. She observes the traits he values, the behavior that evokes his support or his disdain, and the way he treats them. A father's treatment of his wife especially influences the adolescent daughter in her struggle to determine the ways in which she should be similar to, or different from, her mother." [Barbara says:]

> For my father, a woman has to look perfect. She has no brains. My mother has to go to my dad's functions and she has to just sit there with a smile on her face and look great. My father loves it that his wife looks so much younger than everybody else. I don't think they were ever friends. They were just kind of physically attracted to each other. She does everything to please my father. She would go on a diet for my father. She colors her hair for my father. She lies out in the sun all summer—she wants to be as tan as she can for him. . . . And, my father would get in fights because her toenails weren't painted and she was wearing open-toed shoes!

Barbara did not escape her father's criticism of her own body. As a preadolescent she was taller than the other girls in her class, and this made her feel "big."

When I was little my dad always used to make fun of me. I was never fat, just tall, but he used to pinch my stomach and say, "Barbie, you got a little rubber tire in there."

So Barbara stopped eating in the seventh grade.

I lost so much weight they were going to send me to a hospital, because I refused to eat. I wanted to be thin and I loved it. I ate the minimum, a little bowl of cereal for breakfast. I remember my father forcing me to eat a bowl of ice cream. I was crying and he said, "You're going to eat this, you know," which was funny because he's the one who used to call me fat. I used to lie down every night on my bed to see how my hip bones stick out.

When my father said, "You're even skinnier than your sister" I was so happy. It was like an accomplishment; finally for once in my life I was thinner than my sister. I remember going shopping with her to get jeans. I tried on size zero and they fell off. It was the best feeling I'd ever had in my entire life. I went back to school weighing under 90 pounds and I was about 5'6". I loved competitive sports, so when I couldn't play tennis anymore because I was fainting, I started eating. I could eat and get on the scale and I wouldn't even gain any weight because I was playing so much tennis. My eating was normal during that period, the eighth grade. But I wouldn't eat in front of anyone.

Then Barbara started bingeing and vomiting.

It was awful. It was the worst feeling. You know you are about to throw up but you have to get the last bite in. My bingeing would only happen when I was alone, before my parents came home.

I still binge and I always do the exact same thing. I put on my backpack and go to the local food store. I don't want to talk to anybody. I always get cookies, cake, and ice cream because it is easy to throw up. Once I stole from the cafeteria because I was too embarrassed to buy it. The minute I get back to my room, I lock the door. I can't throw up in my bathroom because other girls will hear, so I turn on the music and throw up in a garbage bag. It's so gross. After I throw up I feel awful—it can be so exhausting all you do is fall asleep.

Dieters know severe food restriction over time may trigger an uncontrollable binge.

For Barbara, there was no escaping the pressure to be thin and attractive, "because, that's what my father thinks and likes. I guess I want to live up to his standard." Yet she knew how devastating this had been for her mother and how rocky a relationship her parents had. . . .

Barbara's response to these pressures was a full-blown clinical eating disorder, accompanied by classic psychological symptoms like maturity fears. Afraid of growing up and facing what her mother experienced as an adult married woman, Barbara used compulsive eating to numb her anxiety and anger and purging to relieve her dread of being fat and unloved.

Just as every family's story is unique, there is no single factor that would explain how families induct their daughters into the Cult of Thinness. Some parents go out of their way to *avoid* emphasizing body image issues with their daughters. However, the college women I interviewed were quick to point out the little ways their families passed on the cultural message.

Nearly all of the women I studied felt college life had a profound impact on their body image and eating patterns. They are not alone: Colleges and universities across the country are reporting dramatic increases in eating disorders. Several studies on anorexia nervosa in college populations report that it affects between 6% and 25% of female students. Bulimia ranges between 1% and 19%, and between 23% to nearly

85% engage in binge eating. Although the disorders are listed as separate, the symptoms overlap. While self-starvation is specific to anorexia, obsessive concern with weight and reliance on extreme diet measures is common to both, and bulimic episodes are common among anorectics. "Bulimarexia" describes the mix of symptoms. "Researchers have suggested as many as 19% of college coeds have one form of eating disorder or another" and "subclinical forms of eating pathology [are] generally estimated to be five times more common than the full blown syndromes."

There are several reasons why the college environment may be a breeding ground for weight obsession and the development of culturally induced eating problems. First, college campuses are middle- and upper-middle-class enclaves—a group that places a high premium on thinness in women. With the spread of mass media, especially television and magazine advertising, the Cult of Thinness as a prominent cultural message has reached across the class/race spectrum. As more and more women from working class or ethnic backgrounds populate a wide range of colleges and universities, they become increasingly vulnerable to this message. The Cult of Thinness has spread far beyond the stereotypical eating-disordered cohort of upper-middle-class, white, heterosexual, American adolescent girls.

The stress and strain of college . . . magnifies female students' problems with weight because women often use food as a means of calming or coping.

Second, college life provides an enclosed environment, and this tends to amplify sociocultural pressures. Disorderly eating can spread through imitation, competition, or solidarity. Some researchers note that bulimia is an "acquired pattern of behavior," or suggest that there is a "social contagion" phenomenon that occurs in such an environment. In her book, *The*

Beginner's Guide to Eating Disorder Recovery, social worker and eating disorders specialist, Nancy Kolodny, notes that a type of desensitiz[ation] to the problem of bulimia and anorexia may occur when students are in such a semi-enclosed environment. Kolodny contends, "When people are in close contact socially and emotionally, they can learn the rationale and techniques of bingeing and purging from one another." Another important factor is the importance of an attractive physical appearance in dating. Students who live in close quarters, such as dorms or sororities, often feel pressured to live up to group standards of beauty even if it means engaging in eating-disordered behavior. It follows that schools that emphasize the dating scene may also have higher rates of bulimia.

Peer Group Culture Proves Important

A recent study of female college students followed a group of 23 women at two universities, one predominantly white and the other historically and predominantly black. Over time, these women "shifted more and more of their interests and energy away from college work and toward the peer group, with its emphasis on romance." The authors of the study concluded that the peer group culture was of primary importance to college-age women. This culture centered around how to meet and attract the opposite sex—what the researchers term getting a grade on the "sexual auction block." How attractive a woman could be to men depended on looking good and maintaining a thin body. *This was the primary determination of her status within a peer group.* Academic studies were not highly valued by peer group culture and did not play an important role in the day-to-day college life of these women.

The stress and strain of college, from academics to social life, magnifies female students' problems with weight because women often use food as a means of calming or coping. Weight gained during college is especially detrimental in a climate already primed to value thinness. Extra pounds lead to efforts to lose, which trigger a new round of disorderly eating. This becomes a vicious cycle: stress leading to overeating, leading to weight gain, leading to restricted eating or over-exercising, leading to more stress if the diet or exercise does not work. Even if it does work, just worrying about how to keep the weight off can trigger more eating, more weight gain and so on. . . .

In summary, disorderly eating is not a sign of psychopathology, but a strategy that is a "normal" part of the female existence. In a culture where obesity is becoming more and more common, it becomes increasingly easy to mock the seriousness of the disease.

While psychological trauma or even biochemical deficits may contribute to some of the eating problems occurring in the young college women I have described, psychological and biological theories fail to address the more general issues. The link between the cultural norms of thinness and a young woman is mediated by her family, school, and peer group, who, more often than not translate and embellish society's thinness messages.

4

The Connection Between Shame and Bulimia

Sheila M. Reindl

Sheila M. Reindl is a psychologist at Harvard University's Bureau of Study Counsel. She also practices as a psychotherapist in Cambridge, Massachusetts.

People with bulimia often suffer an overwhelming sense of shame that arises out of unfulfilled or negative relationships with their parents. The mothers and fathers of bulimics have been described as emotionally neglectful, under-involved, or hypercritical in the psychological lives of their children. In such families, the expression of truly held emotions is frowned upon. This leads the young person to feel that their core yearnings and needs are invalid. When an eating disorder arises in these individuals, the parents often refuse to acknowledge that there is a real problem, leaving the young person feeling even more invalidated, shameful, and distrustful of their true feelings.

The [bulimic] women's accounts suggest that once they had developed an internalized sense of shame about themselves early in their lives, within the context of the family, they were especially vulnerable to later experiences of overwhelming shame in contexts beyond the family. Situations that might provoke minimal or manageable shame in most people left them feeling devastated. Each woman describes childhood experiences that appear to have led to an internalized sense of

Sheila M. Reindl, *Sensing the Self: Women's Recovery from Bulimia.* Cambridge, MA: Harvard University Press, 2001, pp. 18–25. Copyright © 2001 by Sheila M. Reindl. All rights reserved. Reproduced by permission of Harvard University Press.

shame, and each marks the onset of her disorder with precipitating experiences in adolescence that evoked a profound sense of inadequacy. I draw upon the experiences of Beth and Gita to illustrate this sequence.

Girls Lacked Parental Attention

Beth grew up in a family of four girls and felt there was never enough attention to go around. She did not receive from her parents confirmation that she was already, inherently enough:

All through high school, I'd danced and run. On Saturday mornings, I would teach dance classes all morning. And then my dad would pick me up and bring me to a track meet. And then I'd run two or three races, long-distance races in the track meet. And my track coach would tell me I should quit dancing and just do track. And my dance teacher would tell me I should quit track and just do dancing. And I couldn't quit either one. So I would do that every Saturday.

I think I used to have like miniature mental breakdowns. 'Cause I wrote for the school newspaper, and I taught dancing on Tuesdays and Saturdays, I ran track every day. My senior year, I was Latin Club president. Every night of the week, I was doing something. I became a lifeguard. It was like, no matter what I did, my parents would say, like my mom'd say, "Well, why don't you become a lifeguard?" And I'd be like, "Okay, I'll be a lifeguard. Sign up for licensing." And I took CPR.

You name it, I've done it in my life. I've taken Irish dancing, Scottish dancing. I took guitar lessons, bagpipe lessons. I competed in all these competitions with dancing. And also in track, I would go away for weekends and stuff. And write for the school newspaper. And I was being tutored twice a week, in math and in chemistry. I was confirmed, so we had to go to confirmation classes. So every single night of the week, I'd be out doing something. And my parents didn't think there was anything weird about it. They just thought you should do that. And I remember one night, just crying, I couldn't stop crying.

Beth's long list of activities indicates her inability to sense when enough was enough. Although her parents did not explicitly tell her she had to do more, she learned that their admiration depended upon her activities and accomplishments.

My father was so judgmental of therapy. The only people who were in therapy were nuts. And it was like a moral weakness. . . . I felt like my parents didn't want me to get help.

Beth recalls an incident of invalidation by her father:

My track coach used to say to me, "Your father puts so much pressure on you." And I'd be like, "No he doesn't." 'Cause he never said "You have to do this" or "You have to do that." But I do remember my freshman year of high school, one of the first races that I ever ran. I came in second. And I was pretty proud of myself. I remember feeling really good about it. . . . I thought he was gonna say, "Good job!" And I remember him saying, "Oh, maybe if you lost five pounds, you'd win next time." And I remember, I was devastated. . . . I just remember being really devastated by it.

Her father's criticism of an experience in which Beth took pride made her feel shame. She had hoped he would share in her sense of triumph and mastery. But instead she heard him say, "It is not good enough." He also communicated that her body was not good enough. In the face of such chronic invalidation, she felt that "I, Beth, am not good enough." She began bingeing at age 12 and purging at age 14.

Beth's early experiences at college reinforced her feeling of inadequacy:

When I went away to college, I had a hard time because it was an Ivy League school, and I felt really inadequate. All these people had had computers, and I never had, I didn't know the first thing about computers. . . . And I didn't go on a freshman trip—most people go on a freshman trip—because I was afraid. I was afraid to go on a trip in the woods with ten people I didn't know . . . I was too afraid, and I thought, "I won't know anybody." And my whole life, I had had friends who I had known since kindergarten. And so I just didn't go. And my father was all upset that I didn't go. 'Cause he was like, "Oh, that's one of the big experiences at the college" and stuff: So he sent in my registration late, but it was too late to sign up. So. And then everybody at school either knew friends from prep school or else knew people from their freshman trip. And I didn't know anybody. And it was really, really hard.

What was shame-inducing and shame-intensifying for Beth was not only being at college with people who seemed more comfortable and competent than she felt but also her father's lack of attention to her emotional experience. He did not acknowledge her fears, much less legitimate them or empathize with them. Instead, he acted as if her fears did not exist (were not real), should not exist (were not legitimate), and were not worthy of concern (did not matter). By his inattention and criticism he created a barrier where Beth had hoped for a bridge. Her eating disorder became markedly more severe during college.

Beth's Parents Refuse to See a Problem

Beth remembers many instances of being unable to evoke her parents' acknowledgment that something was wrong. Her bulimic symptoms got so out of control that her counselor recommended to the college dean that she be required to take a medical leave of absence. She left school, returned to her parents' home, and saw a therapist who referred her to an inpatient program. She attributes her failure to pursue the referral to her parents' attitude: "My father was so judgmental of therapy. The only people who were in therapy were nuts. And it was like a moral weakness. If you were, you were totally cracked ... I felt like my parents didn't want me to get help."

My parents had often said to me, 'Never be selfish.' 'If you think about yourself, you're selfish.'

As her bulimic symptoms worsened, she felt more and more desperate. The night after her twenty-first birthday she overdosed on her antidepressant medication. Even the overdose failed to elicit an acknowledgment of her need for help. The emergency room clinicians focused on assessing her risk of suicide and did not respond to her effort to communicate that she needed care for her eating disorder: "They're just looking at me, 'Well, do you still wanna do it?' And I know if I say to them, 'Yes,' they're not gonna let me go. So I'm like, 'No, no, no. It was all a mistake.' And they're like, 'Well, why did you do it?' and I'm like, 'Well, I'm bulimic.' And they had no concept of what that meant. It was like they were so cold and noncompassionate and just clinical. It almost felt like they were typing it into a typewriter. I just remember feeling, 'What a joke.'"

Her parents, too, refused to acknowledge her need for help. Beth describes the morning after her overdose:

My mom came in and was like, "Are you going to work?" And she wanted to know if I'm gonna go to work that day. I couldn't believe it. I'd just taken a bottle of pills, been in a psychiatric ward all night, and she's waking me up two hours later to see if I'm gonna go to work. I'm like, "Mom, I don't think so." And she's like, "Well, you're not gonna go to work?" I was working at a day camp as a counselor, and I was dating this guy, he was a lawyer, he was like 28, and I was working for his father. And she was like, "What's Dan's father gonna think?" and all this stuff. "What are you gonna tell them?" And I'm like, I just couldn't believe that.

As Beth's story, illustrates, repeated refusals by the important people in one's life to acknowledge one's emotional experience can lead to an ever deepening sense of shame, illegitimacy, and ineffectualness and eventually to desperation and rage.

When she no longer felt adequate, Gita stopped consulting her internal experience.

Gita, age 31 and an elementary school teacher, when asked about her experience of recovering, describes having had, then lost, and then reclaimed a sense of self:

I think the bottom line was learning to trust—and I use that word a lot, I know—myself, my feelings, and my body, and me. I think I lived a lot of my life very outwardly. I tried to please people all the time around me and never thought of myself. I thought that was the way to be. My parents had often said to me, "Never be selfish." "If you think about yourself, you're selfish." "If you do things for yourself, you're selfish." "If you spend money on yourself, you're selfish." And I think I had really overly absorbed that and felt that anything I did for me or listened to me or was focused on me was selfish. And then finally I realized that I couldn't be good to anyone, or myself, or anything unless I did care and sort of grow that center of self.

Do you feel like you had to grow it, like it wasn't—?

Yeah. I had killed it. I had denied it. I had tortured it. I had hated it. I hated it, I hated it, I hated it.

Do you know why?

Many, many reasons, but I think part was not being perfect. And maybe losing my parents' love for me if I wasn't good. "Good," quote unquote. I don't know.

Did you always hate it?

No. I don't think so. I was thinking about first grade and kindergarten. I was really tough, and I was the leader of the girls in first grade—where you play these tag games, I'd be the leader. And I remember being very strong then. . . . I just was really, I was me then. I remember I was strong, and I didn't really worry so much, and I was really in love with living and myself.

And then, I don't know how it all turned around. We did move when I was 7. But I still was pretty strong at 7. But somehow along the line I just got very shy and very quiet and very worried about what other people thought of me. And if I was doing things right. And I just sort of sunk inside. Or the person who was, who I wanted to be, or who I thought of as myself was sort of way in there surrounded by all this gibbly goosh outside, and I had forgotten about it. I forgot that that was in there. . . .

Gita's Self-haterd Begins at Age Seven

When I ask when she started hating herself, Gita recalls that she still had herself at age 7, and still at age 10. Then she pauses:

What happened when I was 11 and 12? Oh, I switched schools when I was—this is pretty interesting. I switched schools for seventh grade. My mom had gone to this private school, and she really wanted me to go there. So I left the public schools in our town and went to private school in another town. And there I had to work really, really hard, and what I had been able to do in public school I wouldn't get by with that, and I had to really become a hard-driving student. And in some ways now I look back at that as very important. It was a good experience for me 'cause I wasn't motivated to pursue it unless I'd been forced to. But I think then it became clear to me that there was an outward person, I think that's when it started. Maybe, so 11, 12? And then, but still not so bad. I can still, if I think back on those times I still see images of Gita. But starting to fade. And definitely by 15, 14, 15, it, she was going.

When she no longer felt adequate, Gita stopped consulting her internal experience. Her excessive concern with her weight began around age 15. She began bingeing and vomiting when she was a freshman in college.

Someone who approaches adolescence with a fragile sense of self can feel annihilated by shame-inducing experiences in adolescence.

The shame Gita felt as a student in her new school was not interpersonally induced shame but rather the shame attendant to the struggle for mastery. She no longer felt adequate to the task of her schoolwork. But we might ask why she was so easily toppled by that shame. It appears that she, like Beth, had arrived at adolescence with a core sense of shame attributable at least in part to emotional neglect and criticism. Gita's father and mother divorced when she was 2, and she grew up living primarily with her father and stepmother. Her mother suffered from labile [unstable] moods and possibly bipolar disorder. Gita describes everyday instances of emotional neglect and criticism by her father and stepmother that may have led to interpersonally induced shame and, over time, internalized shame:

I was often sent to my room because I was acting like my mother. So being like my mother was a huge flaw, and I was punished for acting like her. And what they meant was I was being hysterical. And not in control of my emotions. . . . I would not be rational. I am not totally rational all the time. And something would happen and I would get upset about it, and I certainly at that point did not have good communication skills about what my feelings were, and so I'd hold things in and then I would sort of blow up. Basically crying and maybe saying things that were extremes, like "Oh, I don't really like coffee cake!" or something. Just sort of extremes about things. My father's extremely rational and logical and orderly, and he's a scientist, and everything has to follow and make sense.

Gita Never Learned to Deal with Emotions

I mention that she was, after all, a child at the time. She explains that being a child didn't keep her younger brother from rationally defending his point of view:

> He could fight back, and I would just crumble. And the minute I would crumble, they just don't deal with tears or wimpiness or whatever—I don't know what you want to call it, but I would call it female behavior. They don't see that as appropriate. So off I go. . . . If they disagreed with me, or if they didn't want me to do something, I would be devastated. I wanted them to want what I wanted. And please them. If they were mad at me for something, then I never handled that well either. I always would crumble again, and then they thought I was weak and hysterical.

It seems that her parents did not help Gita to know her emotional experience and to express her feelings effectively. Having never learned how to regulate, tolerate, and integrate emotional experience, in the face of powerful feelings Gita "would just crumble."

Gita's account, like Beth's, illustrates that someone who approaches adolescence with a fragile sense of self can feel annihilated by shame-inducing experiences in adolescence. When she entered a new, competitive school in which she felt she was not good enough, she tried to become the person she sensed others wanted her to be. When she stopped sensing self and primarily sensed other, she got disoriented and wandered far off the course of healthy self-development.

In college, Gita tried to signal to her parents that she had a serious eating disorder by showing them a project she had done for a course:

My senior year of college I actually did a slide-tape video with one of my good friends about eating disorders. At this point, pretending, or talking as though I wasn't one of them. But I was really heartfelt when I wrote it. It was really "This is me," but—. And then I presented it to my parents, and I said, "Well, I think I have some of these tendencies," and they go, "Oh, no, no, no, no. You're not anything like this." And I just remember falling apart inside that they wouldn't hear what I was saying through the slide-tape, and that they thought I was perfectly okay. That just crushed me. And I think then I took a big dip, too, "Maybe I'm not, maybe I'm just being selfish," and "I really don't have a problem."

Her parents' refusal to acknowledge her eating disorder left her doubting that her problem was real or important and thereby exacerbated her sense of inadequacy.

5

Bulimia Is a Kind
of Self-Harm

Dr. Sharon K. Farber

Dr. Sharon K. Farber is a clinical social worker and is the author of When the Body Is the Target: Self-Harm, Pain and Traumatic Attachments.

Some mental health professionals believe that bulimia and other eating disorders are a kind of self-injury like cutting, burning, and general self-mutilation. Childhood abuse, neglect, and other trauma can lead to bulimia which, like other kinds of self-injury, is an attempt by the individual to deal with emotional problems and make oneself feel better. In particular, the purging aspect of bulimia is seen as a way to relieve tension or anxiety.

David: Good Evening. I'm David Roberts. I'm the moderator for tonight's conference. I want to welcome everyone to HealthyPlace.com. Our topic tonight is "Getting Help For Self-Harm." Our guest is author and therapist, Dr. Sharon Farber. . . . Dr. Farber is a board-certified clinical social worker and author of the book: *When The Body Is The Target: Self-Harm, Pain and Traumatic Attachments.* . . . Dr. Farber maintains that there's an addictive-like nature to self-injury. We're going to be talking about that along with the role that childhood neglect, abuse and other trauma play in self-harm, along with why it's still difficult to find qualified therapists to treat this problem and where you can get help.

Good Evening, Dr. Farber, and welcome to HealthyPlace .com. We appreciate you being our guest tonight. Could you please tell us a little more about yourself and your experience in the area of self-harm?

Dr. Farber: I have been in practice for around thirty years. My interest in self-harm came about when I developed a specialty in treating people with eating problems.

Anorexia and bulimia are not always about vanity. It's not always about wanting to look thin. For many people it is more about emotional pain.

Bulimia and Self Mutilation Are Similar

I came to understand that a lot of people with eating problems, especially those who binge and purge, have problems with self injury (especially picking their skin or scratching themselves, sometimes even more obtrusively through burning). Then I went on to do some original research. I wanted to understand why people who injure themselves may also have some kind of disordered eating, or why people who have disordered eating may injure themselves.

I did research where I compared bulimic behavior with self mutilating behavior for similarities and differences. The similarities were extraordinary. Very powerful. I became fascinated and began treating more patients who self-injured.

I should also tell you, when I use the word *self-injury* or *self-mutilation*, I am also talking about a passive form of self-mutilation, and that includes people who compulsively get their bodies pierced or tattooed or branded.

David: What were the similarities between those with bulimia and those who self-mutilated?

Dr. Farber: Well there were quite a lot of similarities. Both of them seemed to be an individual's attempt to solve emotional problems, to make himself or herself feel better. They really served as a form of self-medication. Just as drug addicts and alcoholics use drugs or alcohol in order to medicate themselves, in order to calm themselves down or to rev themselves up, they use self-mutilation to make themselves feel better.

I wanted to understand why people who injure themselves may also have some kind of disordered eating.

I came to regard both the binging and purging and the self-injury as functioning as someone's drug of choice. I found that the self-injurious behavior and the bulimic behavior, especially the purging (which is the most painful part of that experience), were being used as an attempt to release tension or to interrupt or end a feeling of depression or extreme anxiety.

David: In the introduction, I mentioned that you believe there's an addictive nature to self-harm. Can you elaborate on that, please?

Good Feeling Does Not Last

Dr. Farber: Sure, what happens is that a person may start out scratching at their skin or pulling off scabs. It starts out, usually, in a milder form, possibly in childhood, and tends to, for the time being, make the person feel better. The problem is that it doesn't last—the feeling better. So what happens is then they have to do it again-and-again; just as an alcoholic becomes an alcoholic. He develops a tolerance for the alcohol, so he has to drink a greater quantity and much more frequently. The same thing happens with the self-injurious behavior. So someone who starts as picking at the skin, then turns to mild cutting, which then becomes more wild and severe. In other words, they develop a tolerance for the self-injury, so they have to up the ante and do it more severely.

One of the things that I have found that was very interesting has to do with symptom substitution. That is, if somebody tries to give up their self injury but they are not psychologically ready, but they are doing it to please somebody (a boyfriend, parent, therapist), what will happen is another self-destructive symptom will crop up in its place.

One of the things that I have found in my study that was very, very interesting is that both the cutting and the purging (very, very painful and violent) seem to have the same kind of strength as a form of self-medication. Both are extremely powerful, and so often people will react as if they took instant or immediate-acting Prozac. It's that powerful as a form of self-medication and that is why it tends to be so addictive. Of course, it means that if they need something so powerful to make themselves feel better, getting into treatment with a therapist that is knowledgeable and understands how the self-harm behavior works is very, very important. The right kind of treatment can help enormously.

David: We have several audience questions on what we've discussed so far. Let's get to those and then we'll continue with our conversation.

Detached9: Why do you think self-injury is so common in people with anorexia or bulimia? Possibly punishment?

Cutting and purging . . . seem to have the same kind of strength as a form of self-medication.

Bulimia Can Be About Punishment

Dr. Farber: Well the fascinating thing is that punishment is one of the functions it can serve, but for many people it's a form of their body's speaking for them. In other words, the body says for the person what they cannot allow themselves to say or know in words. It's about speaking about emotional pain that they cannot put into words, so their body speaks for them. If you want to think of the bleeding as a form of tears that they couldn't cry, I think that's a good metaphor.

It can be about punishment. Punishing one's self or punishing another. It can be about ridding themselves of something bad or evil inside. A form of cleansing or purifying themselves, except, of course, it doesn't work. If it did work, they would only do it once and they would be sufficiently cleansed or purified.

It starts as someone's solution to an emotional problem, but the solution can become more problematic than the original problem. The solution can take on a life of its own, and become like a runaway train. One of the psychological problems with self harm is that it creates, for the person, a sense of being in control but then it becomes very out of control.

Children can be traumatized by being constantly or chronically neglected.

Cissie_4233: But anorexics and bulimics deal with a certain amount of vanity, therefore why are they now concerned with the scarring?

A Link Between Bulimia and Self-Injury?

Dr. Farber: Well because anorexia and bulimia are not always about vanity. It's not always about wanting to look thin. For many people it is more about emotional pain. And for many people who have a problem with eating they have difficulty with using words to express their emotional pain. So when someone says "I feel fat," they really mean "I feel anxious" or "I feel depressed" or "I feel lonely." For many people with eating problems, the obsession with their physical appearance is just a cover for much deeper emotional pain.

David: I just want to clarify one thing. You are saying that there's a link between eating disorders and self-injury. But, of course, there are people who self-injure who don't have an eating disorder. What about them? Why have they turned to self-injury to cope with their emotions?

Dr. Farber: What I have found in my study is that the people who have suffered the most trauma in their lives, especially childhood trauma (and that trauma can be the trauma of physical or sexual abuse, or children who suffer through various medical or surgical procedures), may need to use more than one form of self harm.

Sometimes trauma is not the dramatic kind of trauma that I have just mentioned. It can be loss, like a child suffering the loss of a parent or grandparent in childhood. Children can be traumatized by being constantly or chronically neglected (either emotionally or physically or both). . . .

David: I want to address the treatment of self-injury, Dr. Farber. What does it take to recover from self-harm?

Dr. Farber: Well, first of all I think it takes a lot of courage. I think it also takes a relationship with a therapist in which you feel really safe—And this feeling of safety doesn't have to start right from the beginning of therapy.

Most people who harm themselves come into therapy feeling very suspicious or wary of the therapist, but over time a sense of trust develops and the patient feels the therapist is not trying to control her (but when I say *her*, I am speaking of my own experiences, where most people who do this are female. Please understand when I say *her*, I mean *her* or *him*). I think when you are in therapy, you need to feel in control of yourself and that your therapist isn't trying to control you or insisting you stop hurting yourself. That is a good start. What can be very helpful is if a therapist can try to help you make it less dangerous (through medical help).

People who hurt themselves tend to have relationships with others that are very painful.

Also, it helps if a therapist can let someone know, right from the beginning, that even if you can't articulate in words why you are doing what you are doing, you must have good reasons for doing it. I think in good therapy, the patient and therapist work together to try to understand how and why self injury became necessary in your life. When you do that, you can try to find other ways to make yourself feel better that are not so harmful—ways that can make you feel better about yourself, ways that you don't have to hide. And I think while all of this is going on, you start to have more control over yourself than you thought, and you find you are more able to speak about the pain that you are feeling inside than you thought, and you don't need to cut yourself or burn yourself so much in order to express that.

David: Are you saying that one method of treating self-injurious behavior is to taper off; sort of like quitting smoking cigarettes, where you smoke lower nicotine cigarettes or use nicotine substitutes until you finally quit?

Dr. Farber: I am not suggesting anything about how they do it. I think when people feel understood, they start to understand the how and why of why they felt the need to hurt themselves and they'll find other ways to make themselves feel better and the self injury quite naturally diminishes.

Treatment of the Person, Not Just Symptom

You see, when I talk about treatment, I am not talking about a treatment of just the symptom (the self injury), I am talking about a treatment of the person who has that symptom.

I think, very often, that people who hurt themselves tend to have relationships with others that are very painful, where they really cannot trust other people and I think that when someone can start to feel really safe in a therapeutic relationship, really safe with the therapist, that this attachment with the therapist, this relationship, can even become stronger than the relationship to self harm, than the relationship to pain and to suffering.

David: Then what you are saying is: that until the person can work through their psychological issues, it is very difficult to control the self-injury.

Dr. Farber: I am saying that people need to do both at the same time. They kind of work together, both understanding how and why the need for self injury arose. Therapists can help their patients find ways to control the self harm behavior. One way I find extremely effective is when they are feeling the impulse to hurt themselves, if they can try just to delay it for five or ten minutes. During those five or ten minutes, pick up a pencil and start to write. Try to put into words what you are feeling. In the process of doing that, in the process of using words to put shape or form into the pain you are feeling inside, the pain inside starts to diminish and by the time you finish writing, the urge to hurt yourself may well be much, much less. It's a way of starting to use your mind to deal with the pain rather than to use your body to deal with the internal pain, and that's the key to recovering from a life of self injury.

6

Athletics Can Contribute to Bulimia

Christa Case

Christa Case is a frequent contributor to the Christian Science Monitor.

Some athletes in competitive sports such as gymnastics suffer from bulimia. Their motivation arises from a desire to achieve a top physical form, impress judges, and increase their efficiency in their demanding sport. The qualities that characterize a top athlete—dedication and willingness to sacrifice for a long-range goal—make these individuals capable of starving or purging themselves. Many athletes in sports that require weighing in get in line with a team's group-think about weight and will do anything to conform to this weight-focused culture.

She was running more than 100 miles a week, a skinny girl in shorts and a sportsbra, with the endurance of the Energizer bunny. At the peak of her collegiate career last year, Anna posted some of the fastest 5-kilometer and 10-kilometer times among Division III NCAA [National Collegiate Athletic Association] competitors nationwide. But during this time, the young athlete (whose real name is withheld to protect her privacy) struggled quietly with an eating disorder. Eventually, bulimia affected her performance—and her times slowed markedly.

As any Olympian could attest, top physical form is a must—and it requires strict regimentation of everything from training schedules to diet. But for some elite athletes, like Anna, the drive for a lithe, lean body results in an obsessive preoccupation with food and body image that can lead to eating disorders.

A Growing Concern

Concern has been highest in women's gymnastics, a sport where 59 percent of competitors have eating disorders, according to one 1994 study. But elite athletes in other sports grapple with eating disorders too—in an effort to present judges with toned, streamlined physiques, or to maximize efficiency in endurance events, or to qualify for certain weight categories. Awareness of the problem is growing, but few sports are taking vigorous, systematic steps to counteract it.

New evidence indicates that eating disorders may be more prevalent among athletes than in the general population. A study in the late 1990s of all elite Norwegian athletes found that 20 percent of the women had an eating disorder, compared with 9 percent of the Norwegian populace, the *Clinical Journal of Sport Medicine* reported in 2003. The study also found that men competing in endurance sports or weight-class events showed a high prevalence of eating disorders.

"The ability to work toward a goal, to sacrifice present satisfaction for future reward, is what makes you good at athletics . . . and good at starving yourself," says Angela Guarda, assistant professor of psychiatry at Johns Hopkins Medical Institutions.

Many experts agree that the very attributes that produce athletic success—notably strict discipline and perfectionism—can also lead to eating disorders such as anorexia (severely curtailing food intake) or bulimia (bingeing and purging). In both cases, affected athletes become obsessed by what they eat and how they look.

"You'll do anything, you'll go to extremes to just keep doing whatever's working," explains Anna. The more weight she lost, the faster she ran. Though there were some danger signs, such as cessation of menstruation, she was convinced that her eating habits were the key to better results.

In sports like wrestling and lightweight rowing, where competitors weigh in before each contest, "group think" may also help promote unhealthy eating patterns. If a majority of athletes on a team take drastic measures to qualify for low weight categories, a culture develops that perpetuates the problem, says Dr. Antonia Baum, a psychiatrist at George Washington University Medical Center. Once eating disorders become part of the culture of a sport, she adds, it is hard to persuade individuals of the need to change their behavior.

The problem is not new in athletics.

Awareness of the problem among coaches varies widely, and whether an athlete gets help may depend largely on the perceptivity of a coach or trainer.

"As far as we can tell, the focus on dieting, body image, and resulting disordered eating has been around for quite some time," says Elizabeth Applegate, author of *Encyclopedia of Sports and Fitness Nutrition.* "The issue is that so many athletes—as little as 10 years ago—didn't talk to their coaches about it."

Figuring It Out and Taking Action

When Anna's coaches finally spoke to her about her weight loss and eating habits, she was not receptive. "Nobody could have said anything to make me stop. I had to figure it out for myself." Though she would throw up most of what she ate, she didn't think she was doing anything wrong.

Finally, Anna reached a crisis. "I got to the lowest low and I just thought, 'I can't do this.' Unfortunately, that's what had to happen for me to realize what was going on."

She has started working with a new coach—one who'd been an elite athlete herself and who'd also battled an eating disorder. "I really listened to her, and it just clicked then. [What she was saying] made so much sense to me." Now, Anna's running has improved and she says she feels better than ever.

USA Gymnastics, the US Women's Tennis Association, and UK Athletics (Britain's track and field association) are among the groups with coaches' education programs to help stem eating disorders. But awareness of the problem among coaches varies widely, and whether an athlete gets help may depend largely on the perceptivity of a coach or trainer.

When it comes to her athletes and food, head coach Suzanne Yoculan takes a forthright but sensitive approach. She discusses "food obsession" frequently with gymnasts on her women's team at the University of Georgia, which has won several NCAA championships. She also requires each one to stay within six pounds of her target competition weight—and if an athlete goes above or below that 12-pound limit, she is not allowed to practice with the team.

Ultimately, the athletes themselves need to take responsibility for maintaining a physique that can execute gymnastic feats, says Ms. Yoculan. "If they can't handle [that responsibility], they shouldn't be in the sport."

7

Eating Disorders Also Impact Older Women

Siri Agrell

Siri Agrell is a writer for the Toronto Globe and Mail.

Eating disorders like bulimia usually affect young women in their teens and early twenties but more women in their thirties, forties, fifties, and beyond are being diagnosed. Some of these women have had eating disorders earlier in their lives and experience recurrences of the disease during midlife. Others develop this problem for the first time as older adults. Unlike their younger counterparts, older women with eating disorders do not exhibit typical symptoms; younger women tend to starve themselves or make themselves throw up while older women instead tend to overexercise or diet constantly. While bulimia is dangerous for all ages, older bodies are harder to recover.

Every day, Helen Engel-Gray makes sure she consumes less than 1,500 calories.

She calculates the fat, protein and carbohydrate content of each morsel that passes through her lips, and if she eats something unhealthy, she tells herself angrily that she deserves to be overweight.

The 31-year-old became anorexic as a teenager, when she ate so little that her hair fell out and her menstrual cycle stopped. "I do not consider myself recovered," the Edmonton [Ontario, Canada] teacher said via e-mail. "I don't know if it is possible to completely revamp the way I look at food."

Siri Agrell, "Eating Disorders in Adult Women on the Rise," *Globe and Mail*, Toronto, ONT: June 21, 2007. Copyright © 2007 Globe Interactive, a division of Bell Globemedia Publishing, Inc. Reprinted with permission from The Globe and Mail.

55

Eating Disorders in Older Women on the Rise

Ms. Engel-Gray is one of a rising number of women past their teens and 20s who have a dysfunctional relationship with food. Some, like her, suffer relapses of eating disorders they faced as teens, while others develop a problem for the first time in their 30s, 40s, 50s or even 60s.

In the public eye, eating disorders have been traditionally viewed as falling into two categories—anorexia and bulimia—that affect a population of girls and women too young to know better. The issue brings to mind visions of body-image obsessed teens and gaunt fashion models, who most people assume suffer, get treatment, grow up and move on.

But health professionals say eating disorders are not just the domain of the young, and that more adult women are now displaying symptoms. This fall, Sheena's Place—an eating-disorder support centre based in Toronto—plans to create a new group for professionals over the age of 25, responding to an increase in calls from adult women.

"We're seeing a trend of older women coming in the last couple of years," said Anne Elliott, the centre's programming director. "The age range is quite phenomenal in our groups. It could be somebody who's 16 or somebody who's 60."

The dangers of eating disorders are serious at any age, but older women can suffer major complications from the bone loss and cardiovascular stress that arises from malnutrition.

Older Women Face New Challenges

According to science journalist Trisha Gura, whose book *Lying in Weight: The Hidden Epidemic of Eating Disorders in Adult Women* was released in May, the number of women older than 30 seeking treatment for eating disorders has tripled in North America over the past 15 years.

A study by the Harvard Eating Disorders Center in Boston followed 240 women for 15 years, from the age of 25 to 40, and found more than two-thirds did not recover from their disorder.

"Older women, those past their 20s, need to know that they are indeed vulnerable to eating disorders and that their illnesses, over time, present a very different challenge than the eating disorders of adolescence," writes Ms. Gura, who realized in her 40s that her own battle with body image was far from over.

Differences Between Adolescence and Adulthood

Part of the problem, she says, is that most adult women do not display typical symptoms of anorexia or bulimia. They do not starve themselves completely or make themselves throw up, but instead exercise compulsively and diet constantly.

Ms. Gura realized she had a major problem alter having her first child. She gained only 10 pounds before giving birth to a 6-pound, 9-ounce daughter.

As is often the case with their younger counterparts, older women's disordered eating habits are triggered by a life transition.

With adults, this could be the loss of a parent, a child moving away, a pregnancy or a divorce.

The aging process alone can also set off a problem with food, Ms. Elliott said.

"Being an older woman is yet another life transition, so with all of us baby boomers going into this, we may be more at risk and the older body is harder to recover," she said.

Facing Major Physical Danger

The dangers of eating disorders are serious at any age, but older women can suffer major complications from the bone loss and cardiovascular stress that arises from malnutrition.

Merryl Bear, director of the National Eating Disorder Information Centre, said adult eating disorders are a relatively new phenomenon, but are easy to understand.

"Self-control, willpower, taking control of one's body: The behaviours that get exhibited by an individual with an eating disorder are strongly admired and sanctioned in our society," Ms. Bear said. "People say, 'You look so young for your age, you're in such good condition, gosh, I admire that you can say no to the slice of cake.'"

Shirley Leon, a clinical counsellor based in Vancouver, has treated many adult women with self-diagnosed eating disorders.

Most focus on their weight as a way of coping with stress, she said, as the responsibilities of adult life pile up. "They have to be family people and career people," she said.

Many of her clients seek help because they are pregnant, or are trying to get pregnant, she said, and realize they can no longer be purging and excessively exercising.

Eating Disorder or Maintaining Their Figures?

But Ms. Engel-Gray knows plenty of women who have not sought help for their obvious issues with food.

She describes friends who regularly binge eat to the point of pain, "and then work out like demons to try to burn off the calories that they have consumed."

She has seen colleagues obsess over Weight Watchers points or nibble at salad during lunch after skipping breakfast altogether.

"A teenage girl would be accused of having an eating disorder," she said. "I think that perhaps there is an underlying admiration for older women who can maintain their figures . . . even if it's not in a healthy way."

8

The Internet Often Helps
Shape Eating Behaviors

Lynell George

Lynell George is a features staff writer at the Los Angeles Times.

The Internet has made it possible for bulimics and others with eating disorders to find one another in Web sites, chat rooms, and blogs where they give support and advice on the practice of their disease. Despite efforts by hosting sites to close down pro-bulimia and pro-anorexia sites they tend to reemerge elsewhere under other names but still carrying the same message. Attempts by eating disorder specialists to contact the owners of the Web sites in order to convince them to close down have failed. The Webmasters believe it is their right to promote their message and that anyone who visits a pro-eating disorder chat room or blog is doing so at their own risk.

At first, peering into her computer screen, Janice Saunders was struck by the eerie triptychs: jutting hipbones, a blade of clavicle, a rib cage in relief.

A double click brought her to message boards full of wild chatter and ghoulish advice: "Worried about that side of fries last night? Swallow half a bottle of laxatives!" "At a plateau? Try syrup of ipecac, what they use at hospitals for accidental poisoning. This helps to purge the body."

With each left-click, each move of the mouse, a murky world came more clearly into focus.

"It is so great to feel lean and pure and clean. Thats why I'm promoting Anorexia, although I don't think it should be labeled a 'disease.' It's not like that. Ana gives comfort, control, beauty. Everything that a girl could ask for."

Pro-anorexia? Anorexia as a desirable choice? At first, she says, still sounding a bit bewildered, "I thought it was a joke. I thought I was misreading."

But as she explored, Saunders, who has been running her own Web site, Support Concern and Resources for Eating Disorders, or SCARED, out of her home in London, Ontario, found scores of pro-anorexia—"pro-ana"—sites. Deeply disturbing pages aimed at anorexics and bulimics were filled with tips on how to protect tooth enamel from frequent episodes of purging, 2 A.M. "no-excuses" exercise regimes and photos that flaunted a death-camp aesthetic of skin and bones.

Deeply disturbing pages . . . were filled with tips on how to protect tooth enamel from frequent episodes of purging.

Her early explorations became a vigil. Every day she gets up at 4:30 *a.m.* and goes to her computer to track the activity on her site—and the others. The voices haunt her. "I live with Mia, but Ana comes to visit occasionally," says one posting. "I no longer hide Ana from anyone," confesses another.

Within the fluid anonymity of the Internet, a new generation has made its eating disorders a unifying badge and, ultimately, a way to bond in a dangerous pursuit.

"Now I hate Mia and I want Ana more than anything."

A Unifying Badge

"Mia"—bulimia nervosa—and "Ana"—anorexia nervosa—are the two most tenacious eating disorders. Once, many anorexics and bulimics tended to isolate themselves, say experts who have been helping clients wrestle with these complex conditions for decades. But as Saunders discovered, that is beginning to change. Within the fluid anonymity of the Internet, a new generation has made its eating disorders a unifying badge and, ultimately, a way to bond in a dangerous pursuit.

"They see this as something [to be] cherished," Saunders explains. "They tell one another that it is going to give them happiness: It's a place where they can make friends."

Blogs Nurture Visitors' Obsession

In this realm, "support" or "advice" doesn't mean referrals to doctor's care or tips for recovery. Rather, the hundred or so Web logs—or blogs—loops, diaries and online pro-ana communities nurture their visitors' consuming obsession with extreme thinness.

One click away from the "Thin Commandments" is the "Ana Creed": "I believe in Control, the only force mighty enough to bring order to the chaos that is my world." And just a hyperlink away from that are rated lists of "recommended" over-the-counter diet pills, supplements and laxatives. The sites, say eating-disorder experts, pose grave dangers to their most vulnerable visitors and a new set of roadblocks to those who try desperately to treat them.

"Anorexics tend to be a competitive bunch," says Jenn Berman, a Beverly Hills-based therapist who daily sees the eating disorders that take hold arise in the driven athletes and actresses she treats. "So reading that someone lost X amount of pounds just ups their activities. It's one of the reasons that group therapy isn't recommended. Anorexics try to outdo each other—in illness, not in success."

The pro-ana community is well-known to those who work with anorexics and bulimics. Saunders heard about it when a young girl battling an eating disorder visited her SCARED page and told her about the sites she had run into en route.

Saunders was immediately concerned because she knew how powerfully women are drawn to the Internet as they seek self-help tips.

Five years ago, she had launched a Web page to help herself deal with depression and offer a forum to others and was surprised to see how many of her regular visitors sought help with eating disorders. SCARED evolved to support them.

Saunders wanted to see the new pro-ana sites for herself. She took to sitting on a few mailing lists, using names such as SkinnyMini. And in no time she began receiving daily e-mail reminders: "Remember. Do not eat today." Or a nudge to recite one of the Thin Commandments: "Thou shall not look at food."

She jumped in with counter-arguments—sometimes riling others enough to get kicked out of various rooms and lists. Then, last year, she began running across postings that pushed her beyond chat room spats. "One of the girls," she recalls, "was telling girls to cut off the fat off their bodies with a serrated knife! Take a pile of laxatives!'"

Many eating-disorders specialists see shadings of their patients' complex profile in the Webmasters' tenacity.

The mother of four daughters in their early to mid-teens, she asked herself: "Do I want [them] to read this? There are girls who are spending their money and busting their butts to get help, and this is what they are coming across."

Saunders contacted Internet service providers, demanding that the sites be shut down for offering content that harms minors. No response. Eventually, though, her protests, along with those of others who had begun to informally organize on her site, got attention. Last summer, Saunders returned from a vacation to find her online mailbox overflowing with messages, their subject lines rejoicing: "We won!" or "Congratulations! They've closed the sites!' I thought, 'Oh my God! That's great!'"

But in just a few short weeks, the pro-ana pages were back—all over the Internet.

Hyperactive Sites Are Part of the Compulsive Profile of the Eating Disordered

Again and again, under slightly altered names or camouflaged by coded keywords, these sites and their Webmasters rebuild and resurface, sometimes slightly disguised, but each time more emboldened. "They are fighting a losing battle," one Webmaster recently wrote. "I will just keep showing up."

In the United States, the battle was joined by such health care professionals as Holly Hoff, director of programs for the National Eating Disorders Assn., based in Seattle. Her organization's efforts paralleled Saunders', as her group sent letters to Yahoo and other service providers that were hosting the sites. Yahoo took note in August and was the first to begin closing pro-ana sites and clubs, citing their harmful or threatening content. Other service providers followed suit. But again, the sites reemerged elsewhere.

These sites may look amateurish—even harmless. But therapists are already seeing alarming evidence of their effects. Their casual tone and imperfections, like a voice of a friend are, in fact, their power.

Many eating-disorders specialists see shadings of their patients' complex profile in the Webmasters' tenacity.

Frequently, says Hoff, anorexics and bulimics "tend to be women who are perfectionists, goal-achieving. They are the good students, the good child, the good mate, the good friend." So the doggedness fits the profile.

"These sites illustrate an extreme representation of the illness," says Margo Maine, a Connecticut-based therapist and author of *Body Wars: Making Peace with Women's Bodies*. "More than just a diagnosis, it becomes their total identity, this badge of illness."

Extremely Ana, Tiny Dancer, Stick Figures, Only Popular W/ Anorexia, Wanna B Skinny, Thinspiration and Dying for Perfection are just a few Web sites that have recently been shuttered or slipped from plain sight. Of the sites that remain, some are zine-like blogs with a tumble of busy graphics that recall inky notebook doodlings or hasty post-punk cut-and-paste locker collages. Others are crowded chat rooms or hyperlinked Web rings. Compulsion, and a desperate, unattainable desire for control, are everywhere.

"I ate 780 calories the other day and I still feel like I want to die, (I wrote 'fat pig' on my left leg in marker, that seemed to help a bit), so I went home and went running at 2:30 *a.m.* About 7 miles I try to maintain a sense of balance."

Sites May Only Look Amateurish

With their misspellings, muddy graphics or stream-of-consciousness entries, some of these sites may look amateurish—even harmless. But therapists are already seeing alarming evidence of their effects. Their casual tone and imperfections, like a voice of a friend, are, in fact, their power.

And that easy intimacy drowns out the concerns of friends, therapists and families in the minds of those with eating disorders.

"Right away you see the skepticism," says therapist Berman, bent over the laptop propped open on her office desk, a page open to Friday night action on one pro-ana site. The boards are alive; postings arrive every few minutes. Their hyperactivity, says Berman, is part of the compulsive profile: Some posts flame a TV drama's depiction of bulimia—sight unseen. Others complain about doctor visits or stew over a concerned husband's attempt to force a meal—"at least a chicken nugget." "There's a real we-versus-them aspect," Berman says. "But all these people want to be thin as opposed to being well."

Indeed, the sites paint "Ana as lifestyle" in vivid brush-strokes: Weight as elegant aesthetic; willpower as mark of strong character.

This sort of argument marks the first phase of the illness, says Ali Borden, primary therapist at the Monte Nido Treatment Center in Calabasas [California]. "When they start in on an eating disorder," says Borden, "they are completely unaware of the effects. They think that they will be thin, loved, successful, popular—which seems to be the stage that the people running the sites are totally locked in. But suddenly they realize: I feel tired, I'm not seeing my friends anymore, I feel weak, I feel sick. But then they think: Well that must mean I'm not working hard enough. I need to work harder."

As they do, they face realities of a body deprived of food. Hair thins. Bones snap. Organs give out.

An estimated 5 million to 10 million American women in post-puberty struggle with some form of eating disorder, says Hoff. And without intervention, Berman notes, anorexia has the highest fatality rate in the DSM-IV, the Diagnostic and Statistical Manual of Mental Disorders published by the American Psychiatric Assn. That's what these sites often gloss over, stresses Berman. "People die from this disease," she says. "They die."

A Blurred Line Between Dieting and an Eating Disorder?

"Sharon," a pro-ana Webmaster, created her site as a refuge from the rub of criticism, the prying questions about her weight and size. Her pages are understated, almost elegant. She says she spends "too many" hours a day tending to them, coordinating a full roster of forums—from fasting and pills to women with families ("How do you balance ana and family life?").

In the mid-'90s, she says, she was 16, discovering the Internet—and obsessed with thinness. "I put up my first page about the beauty of starvation," she says, and mail piled in, both hateful and kind. "I was quite proud of myself causing such a stir!"

"But my interest in this has gone beyond being provocative," she explains. "My original goal . . . was to bring the issue of eating disorders to the forefront by making a site that was 'borderline.'" Where do diets end and anorexia and bulimia begin?

"I think the line is blurry," she says. "In women's mags you see an article about the horrors of pro anorexia, or some ballet dancer who died of an ED [eating disorder] right next to ads for fad diets and bone-thin models. I felt that I was receiving a mixed message from the world around me, so I decided to send one right back."

Experts don't disagree with "Sharon" about the conflicting signals sent to women. "When I begin therapy," Maine says, "I tell patients, 'Our society is like living in a cult, and I'm going to have to deprogram you.'"

A wisp of an Olympic star or blade-thin runway model offered up as symbols of success in one corner of the culture are likely to turn up as well on sites like "Sharon's." Some pro-ana pages are festooned with graphics of the Kate Mosses or Calista Flockharts [ultrathin modles and actresses] of the moment, scanned from fan or glamour magazines. Others might be interspersed with anonymous photos of skeletal girls and women—miming the provocative poses of their idols. Such images (as well as affirmations, rules and revelations) are referred to as "triggers"—inspiration to help extreme dieters stay the course. "Hunger hurts, but starvation works!"

Victoria Jackson understands the power of triggers. Now 20, the University of North Carolina student has wrestled with anorexia since 9. "Being anorexic is really hard, and it takes a ton of self-control and willpower," Jackson says. A message or picture on a Web site, she suggests, "isn't strong enough to convince a mind to do something so demanding. I really think that the decision is already made. But the Web sites are like a morale booster, something to keep you going, to make things easier."

When she looks at the sites at a reporter's request, she remembers the rush that used to accompany a new discovery, a new technique for staying in control of her weight. "A drink that has no calories . . . [or] a . . . new trick to stop hunger pains," she explains, felt like a new chance. "You are going against what your body is telling you. If you're really hungry, that's hard to fight, so new ways to make it easier are embraced. It's just one more thing to be absorbed in. One more thing to drive you, one more tool.

"I'm past all of that," Jackson says, "but even looking at [a site] really upsets me. It's really going to add to people's problems."

Web Site Visits Are Often Kept Secret

While some patients are horrified by the sites and immediately alert their therapists, others don't always let on that they've made visits, says Maine, "but you figure it out." The sites "just reinforce every pathological thought. Some sites tell what to wear. How to mask your lag [in gaining weight]: Weights, shoes under your arms. Eating olives and pickles, water loading. There's a science to it."

At the same time, she adds, they provide fuel for denial. "A lot of these patients will look at these sites and say: 'Well, I've never been that skinny!' or I've not been to the hospital three times. So I'm not really an anorexic. That's just part of the whole web of illogical thinking."

Appealing to the Webmasters

Specialists such as Maine felt their patients pulling away as they spent more time on the sites, but they were reluctant to lead public battles to get pro-ana material off the Internet. "We were worried we'd lead [patients] there," Maine says. So last year, before they turned to the Internet service providers, Hoff and other specialists tried contacting the Webmasters directly.

"We made appeals about their own health and well-being," Hoff says. "We reminded them about their potential for harm. Unfortunately, we didn't have much luck. They felt that it was their right. That people visit at their own risk. Many of them feel that they are martyrs."

They hang on, tenacious.

So does Janice Saunders.

After her success last summer, she was flamed with angry e-mail, pelted with profanity, taunted and threatened. But there have been sweet surprises.

She played a particularly vigorous game of cat and mouse with an angry Webmaster, whose site was shut down, then re-surfaced and was shut down again. It reappeared yet again, but this time, it had changed.

"What are you here for?" the site's most recent version now asked visitors. "What do you hope to find?"

What followed was a sober renunciation and apology that gave Saunders pause. "I am now very grateful to Yahoo for removing my Web site, twice. I was absolutely devastated and angry at the time, now I am very grateful and fully supportive of them. Please reach out. You don't have to be lonely or hurting anymore."

Saunders was stunned, and revitalized. "I can't remove every Web site," she says. "But I think if it changes one thing . . . it's well worth it. Because too often, I'll ask, 'Where's so and so?' They're gone from the lists, the chat rooms. Sometimes there is no answer. They don't know what happened. Some girls just disappear."

9

Antidepressants Are Highly Successful in Treating Bulimics

Diane Mickley

Diane Mickley, M.D., is the founder and director of the Wilkins Center for Eating Disorders in Greenwich, Connecticut. She is also an associate clinical professor in the Department of Psychiatry at the Yale University School of Medicine.

Antidepressant medications, especially selective serotonin reuptake inhibitors (SSRIs), have been found to be successful in the treatment of bulimia nervosa because they improve the function of neurotransmitters, the chemical messengers in the brain. The drug fluoxetine is used as part of cognitive behavioral therapy to help bulimics avoid relapses. Researchers have found that bulimics benefit from fluoxetine even if they are not depressed. Topiramate, a drug developed for the treatment of epilepsy, is also used to treat bulimia nervosa. Although these medications are not widely prescribed for long-term use, some patients may have to take them for more than several months or even a year or two. Side effects of medications for eating disorders are relatively minor and include nausea, headache, fatigue, insomnia, and sometimes agitation and overexcitement. These symptoms usually pass in a week or two.

Anorexia nervosa and bulimia nervosa are associated with altered levels of neurotransmitters, or chemical messengers in the brain. This is particularly true of serotonin levels.

Diane Mickley, "Medication for Anorexia Nervosa and Bulimia Nervosa," *Eating Disorders Today Newsletter*, 2007. www.gurze.com Copyright © 2007 Gurze Books. Reproduced by permission.

It makes sense, then, that medications developed to improve the function of neurotransmitters might be useful in the treatment of eating disorders. Research over more than a decade has shown that medications can indeed be valuable in the treatment of bulimia nervosa. More recent research has shown some promise for the use of medications in treating anorexia nervosa as well.

The Most Widely Studied Medications

Several different categories of psychiatric medications have been shown to be beneficial, but the most widely studied are the SSRIs (Selective Serotonin Reuptake Inhibitors), the first and most famous of which is fluoxetine, or Prozac. Other SSRIs include sertraline (Zoloft), paroxetine (Paxil), fluvoxamine (Luvox), and citalopram/escitalopram (Celexa/Lexapro). All raise the levels of serotonin available in parts of the brain. Venlafaxine (Effexor) is a related drug that raises both serotonin and norepinephrine.

If fluoxetine is going to be helpful, the results will be apparent within 4 weeks.

Though popularly dubbed antidepressants, these drugs are used for a wide array of psychiatric diagnoses, including anxiety, phobias, panic attacks, obsessive-compulsive disorder (OCD), premenstrual dysphoria (PMS), post-traumatic stress disorder (PTSD), and impulse control disorders. Many of these are common additional problems in patients with eating disorders and their families. . . .

Two Successful Treatments

The initial goal for bulimia nervosa is . . . symptom management—in this case, stopping the binge/purge behaviors. Two treatments have been documented by evidence-based scientific studies to have the best short-term success rates. The first is cognitive behavioral therapy (CBT), and the second is high-dose fluoxetine. Results are roughly comparable, with a suggestion that the two together may be better than either one alone. However, since only a quarter of patients achieve symptom remission with these approaches, further treatment is generally needed.

The largest bulimia nervosa treatment trial in the world documented the benefits of high-dose fluoxetine. This led to approval of fluoxetine by the FDA [Food and Drug Administration] specifically for the treatment of bulimia nervosa. Treatment is recommended to begin and continue at a dose of 60 mg [miligrams]. (The dose of 20 mg commonly used for depression was no better than a placebo.) Bulimics benefit from fluoxetine regardless of whether they are depressed. Moreover, if fluoxetine is going to be helpful, the results will be apparent within 4 weeks. At least one study has shown this to be a successful initial approach when used by primary care providers.

Doctors must weigh the risks of the treatment compared to the risks of the illness.

Are other medications in the SSRI category also helpful? Published studies have now shown sertraline to benefit bulimia nervosa at a higher dose range (150 mg). Although clinicians commonly do use other SSRIs for this purpose, the data to assess their benefit and dosage is simply not available. Other classes of antidepressant medications have also been shown to be helpful for the treatment of bulimia nervosa and binge eating disorder.

An Option for Bulimics

Topiramate [is in] a totally different category of medication than was developed for treating epilepsy. It is now commonly used for migraine headaches, and it is an exciting new option for patients with bulimia nervosa, binge eating disorder, and simple obesity. Studies in patients with these disorders show binge reduction, reduced preoccupation with eating, and weight loss. Topiramate is used in relatively low doses (100–200 mg) for eating disorders and weight loss. Gradual initial dose increases are required to avoid mental sluggishness. Other side-effects are common but generally not serious. Patients who are taking hormones, including oral contraceptives, may also require dose adjustment due to interaction with topiramate. Zonisamide is another promising agent in this class.

Continuing progress is being made in understanding the biology of . . . bulimia nervosa.

Minor Side Effects

None of the medications described above have any potential to be addicting. Often their use can be transitional, for several months to a year or two, while recovery progresses and solidifies. However, since eating disorders frequently occur in patients with depression or anxiety disorders, some of these people will benefit from longer-term use of medication.

What about side-effects? As in all medical care, doctors must weigh the risks of the treatment compared to the risks of the illness. Fortunately, most of the side-effects of the medications used for eating disorders are relatively minor, especially compared to the serious dangers of being anorexic or bulimic. . . . The SSRIs may have mild initiation side-effects including nausea, headache, fatigue, or insomnia, and less commonly agitation and over-excitement. These often pass within a week or two but they may persist and should always be discussed with the physician. More enduring side-effects may include vivid dreams, sweating, and a reduction in sexual interest or performance. Medications that leave the body quickly (paroxetine, escitalopram, and venlafaxine) should be tapered off, since sudden discontinuation can produce flu-like symptoms. Recently, the news media has focused on whether teenagers respond as well and safely to SSRIs as adults do. A small percent of adolescents (and a few adults) experience akathisia while taking common psychiatric drugs. Akathisia is a kind of motor restlessness, a feeling of "jumping out of your skin," which should be reported to your physician. In addition, concerns have been voiced about an increased risk of suicide among children and teens taking SSRIs, even though overall suicide rates have dropped significantly as SSRI use has become widespread. Government agencies are currently evaluating this question.

The exciting overview is that continuing progress is being made in understanding the biology of anorexia nervosa and bulimia nervosa, as well as how medications can help. Specialists in the field will be aware of the latest developments and the latest information about the uses and benefits of available medications. The best outcome—ideally, complete recovery—is most likely with an up-to-date and experienced eating disorder team working in firm alliance with the patient and family.

10

Involuntarily Hospitalization Is Effective in Treating Bulimics

MedscapeWire

Researchers at the University of Iowa have found that involuntary treatment of patients with eating disorders such as bulimia nervosa is as effective as voluntary treatment. After reviewing the records of 397 patients at the University of Iowa Eating Disorders Program, researchers found that 66 patients who had been admitted to treatment involuntarily regained lost weight and were able to return home. The involuntary patients did not file lawsuits or complaints about their commitment, an important finding due to the controversial nature of involuntary treatment. The involuntary patients had more hospitalizations than other patients in the study group and were, on the whole, not fully aware of the dangerousness of their situation. The unknown factor remaining in this study is the long-term prognosis for these patients. Some researchers think that involuntary patients may just go along with the treatment in order to be discharged from the program. Once back home, these patients may return to their former ways.

Trying to help a person who doesn't want help for a problem is often an exercise in futility. However, in the case of eating disorders, involuntary treatment seems to be as effective in the short-run as voluntary treatment is.

The observation was made by University of Iowa [UI] researchers in one of the largest investigations to date on the subject and the first study of its kind conducted at the UI. The findings appear in the November 1 [2000] issue of the *American Journal of Psychiatry*.

Accepting Treatment

The researchers reviewed the records of 397 patients (351 women and 46 men) who had been admitted to the University of Iowa Eating Disorders Program over a 7-year period for anorexia, bulimia, or eating disorders not otherwise specified. Sixty-six (16.6%) of the patients received their treatment after involuntary legal commitment. Individuals in this category have refused hospitalization despite the life-threatening severity of their illness but can legally be required to enter a treatment program.

"We found that once admitted, involuntary patients restored weight and were able to return home," said Tureka Watson, a researcher in psychiatry and the study's designer and lead author. "Many of them also said they understood they were sick and needed treatment."

Watson added that while involuntary treatment can be controversial, no detained patient took any legal action or registered any type of complaint. Numerous safeguards are also in place within the state to protect the rights of people committed involuntarily for medical treatment.

It's possible that some patients may be 'eating their way out' of hospitalization just to go back to their ways.

The involuntary patients, which included 60 women and 6 men, were hospitalized on average for 58 days, about 17 more days than the voluntary patients, due to their lower weights on admission. However, both patient groups gained weight at about the same rate on a weekly basis and were otherwise similar in age, sex ratio, and marital status as well as history of substance abuse and depression.

Little Understanding of How Actions Affect Their Lives

The researchers found that the involuntary group of patients had more previous hospitalizations, an indication of their resistance to treatment. They also scored slightly lower on certain tests that measure how well a person understands what is going on around them and how their actions affect their lives. Watson said the difference could be attributed to the lower body weight of those patients.

"They are so starved, their bodies don't function at full capacity," she said. "Whatever energy the body does get goes to maintaining essential functions such as their heart rate and body temperature. We know it becomes more difficult for them to concentrate, for example."

One drawback to the study, Watson noted, is that the researchers do not know how the patients do in the long-term.

"After five years, do the involuntarily treated patients relapse or even die of something related to the eating disorder?" Watson said. "It's possible some patients may be 'eating their way out' of hospitalization just to go back to their ways."

Researchers from the University of Iowa are currently working on that question with researchers from Johns Hopkins University on a long-term study to see how patients do 5 to 20 years after treatment.

A previous study by other investigators showed about 5 years after treatment, mortality for involuntary patients was 12.7% compared with 2.6% for voluntary patients.

11

Behavior Therapy Is Better than Hospitalization for Bulimics

Association for Behavioral and Cognitive Therapies

Behavior and cognitive therapists focus on helping patients deal with the current situation they find themselves in (such as bulimia) rather than the past. They help individuals examine their views and beliefs in order to replace destructive ways of living with ways of living that give individuals more control over their lives. Since eating forms an important focus of family and social life in the United States, it is understandable that our abundance of food and our preoccupation with it leads many persons to develop eating disorders such as bulimia. In treating bulimics, behavior and cognitive therapists advise against hospitalization unless there are medical complications or other associated severe psychological disorders. In fact, they believe that hospitalization may actually hinder recovery because the patient is removed from the environment in which the problem occurs. They argue that bulimics must learn to eat normally in their own environment.

Behavior Therapy is a particular type of treatment that is based firmly on research findings. It aids people in achieving specific changes or goals. Goals might involve:

- a way of acting—like learning to change eating patterns;

- a way of feeling—like helping a person be less depressed;

- a way of thinking—like developing interests other than body image;

- a way of dealing with physical or medical problems—like combining antidepressants and cognitive behavior therapy to best deal with eating disorders and the depression that often accompanies them; or

- a way of coping—like training people to monitor their eating.

Behavior Therapists and Cognitive Behavior Therapists usually focus on the current situation, rather than the past. They concentrate on a person's views and beliefs, about their life, not on personality traits. Behavior Therapists and Cognitive Behavior Therapists treat individuals, parents, children, couples, and whole families.

Replacing ways of living that do not work well with ways of living that work, and giving people more control over their lives are common goals of behavior therapy. . . .

Cognitive behavior therapy has been shown . . . to be helpful in overcoming bulimia.

Eating Is a Focus

Not only do we eat to live, but eating forms an important focus for our family and social lives. Living in a wealthy society, such as the United States, with a relative abundance of food, appears to predispose us to the three major disorders of eating: obesity, bulimia, and anorexia nervosa. . . .

Characteristics of bulimia: Social standards for body shape, particularly for women, change over time. In the United States today, a thin body shape is the prevailing standard for women.

Most women diet from time to time, but a few restrict their diet in a major way. Some of the latter lose control of their eating behavior and begin to binge-eat. Since binge-eating leads to the possibility of weight gain, such individuals then begin to purge, either by inducing vomiting, using laxatives or diuretics, or, less frequently, by not eating for several days.

Over time, an extreme concern about body shape develops, fostering ever more rigid dietary restrictions and an increasing frequency of purging when arbitrary food rules are broken. This complex of behaviors is known as bulimia, and carries with it several health risks. These include an increase in dental problems and a loss of potassium, which may lead to complications such as abnormal heart rhythms. Psychological problems, such as an increased tendency to become irritable and depressed, also occur in this condition. The vast majority of bulimics are women, although a few men do develop this problem.

Unless there are major medical complications, or an associated severe psychological disorder, hospitalization is not usually necessary for the treatment of bulimia.

Treatment: Over the last few years, cognitive behavior therapy has been shown, in carefully conducted research, to be helpful in overcoming bulimia. Treatment consists of careful record keeping, which is used to help the patient acquire new behaviors including:

1. eating three or more balanced meals each day;
2. delaying and then eliminating purging;
3. examining and changing some of the erroneous beliefs regarding food, dieting, and body shape; and
4. eventually learning that accomplishments other than body shape are important to the development of an adequate self-image.

The length of treatment varies with the severity of the problem, although the average number of treatment sessions is between 15 and 20. Most bulimic clients receive some benefit, in terms of enhanced self-control of binge-eating and purging, through the use of cognitive behavior therapy, and about two-thirds are able to resume normal eating patterns. Weight gain after treatment is the exception rather than the rule, and such weight gains are usually small.

Behavior therapy for bulimia nervosa is available at a number of specialized centers, and it is important when selecting a treatment program to evaluate the therapist's experience in treating patients with bulimia. Medication, principally the use of antidepressants, has also been shown to be useful. Such medication may be particularly helpful for patients who do not respond optimally to behavior therapy.

Hospitalization is not necessary: Unless there are major medical complications, or an associated severe psychological disorder, hospitalization is not usually necessary for the treatment of bulimia. Indeed, because hospitalization removes individuals from the environment in which the problem occurs, it may retard recovery from the disorder, since bulimics must learn to eat normally in their own environment.

12

Insurers Should Pay for Bulimics' Hospitalization and Treatment Programs

Elizabeth Bernstein

Elizabeth Bernstein writes on psychology, women's issues, and health-related topics.

Payment for the treatment of eating disorders can be very costly, with fees at inpatient facilities running as high as one thousand dollars per day for a stay of three to nine months. Many insurance companies do not adequately cover treatment programs, thus forcing parents of bulimic children to pay hundreds of thousands of dollars of their own money. These parents are lobbying the insurers to change the rules and extend coverage to persons suffering from eating disorders. Some medical experts are helping parents in their efforts. These experts are saying that, although eating disorders are a form of mental illness, they have a biological core with genetic components. Select inpatient treatment centers, such as the Renfrew Center (located in cities throughout the eastern United States), help families find ways to cover the costs. The only way to achieve a long-term solution is to sue the insurance companies to change the way they decide on coverage.

Mike Hall's daughter, Meghan, has struggled with anorexia nervosa for the past three years. At times, her weight has dropped as low as 67 pounds—she is 5'6" tall—and she has had to be force-fed through a tube. Once, a priest performed last rites.

Elizabeth Bernstein, "Eating Disorders: Families Fight Back: Insurers Have Long Covered Only a Fraction of Huge Costs; Now, Pressure to Pay More," *Wall Street Journal*, January 2, 2007. Copyright © 2007 by Dow Jones & Company, Inc. All rights reserved. Reproduced by permission.

During this time, Meghan, now 23, has been hospitalized for 16 months for her eating disorder and has spent two more months in an intensive outpatient program. Humana, her father's insurance company, covered her for 10 days of hospitalization each year as a mental-health benefit. Her dad was left to pay for the rest—almost $1 million.

"I always thought that insurance would take care of my children if they got sick," says Mr. Hall, 48, who co-owns a telecommunications consulting business in Highland Park, Ill., and has been paying insurance premiums for 25 years. "But when I needed it, I was told, 'Sorry, you don't qualify.'"

Reluctant to Pay

For years, insurance companies have been reluctant to pay for extended treatment for eating disorders, such as anorexia nervosa or bulimia nervosa, claiming they are psychological in nature, not physiological, and should fall under mental-health coverage, which is typically limited.

Humana declined to discuss the details of Mr. Hall's coverage, citing privacy laws. The company says its policies comply with applicable requirements under the law in states where the company operates.

Support groups are . . . encouraging families to become their own advocates.

Many eating-disorder advocacy groups report that they regularly receive calls from patients and families who have exhausted their insurance coverage and have racked up thousands of dollars worth of bills. Marc Lerro, executive director of the Washington, DC–based Eating Disorders Coalition, says he gets about nine calls a week from people seeking advice on how to pay for treatment. "They're spending down their savings, mortgaging their homes, cashing in their retirement accounts," he says.

Now, a growing number of families and patient advocates are fighting back, encouraged by medical expert opinions that say eating disorders, though a mental illness, have a biological component. Dr. Thomas R. Insel, the director of the government's National Institute of Mental Health, wrote in a recent letter to the National Eating Disorders Association, an advocacy group based in Seattle, that anorexia has "a biological core, with genetic components."

In an effort to get insurance carriers to cover these diseases as they would any other biological illness, families and advocacy organizations are filing lawsuits against insurers, forming groups to lobby politicians for new legislation, and teaching other parents how to appeal denied claims.

Assistance to Patients

Treatment centers also are finding ways to help families cover costs. Renfrew Center, which operates eating-disorder treatment facilities in seven states, has contracted with 75 insurance companies around the country to provide at least some assistance to patients. Renfrew, which charges $1,650 a day for inpatient treatment, also offers some scholarships to extend the stay of patients whose insurance has run out. Timberline Knolls, a residential treatment center in suburban Chicago, where inpatient treatment is $875 a day, has hired a full-time financial advocate who works with residents and their families to assess their coverage, mediate with insurance companies to get approval for care, and to help them seek private loans or scholarships.

Experts say only about half of the patients diagnosed with . . . bulimia fully recover.

Support groups are also encouraging families to become their own advocates. The National Association of Anorexia Nervosa and Associated Disorders, based in Highland Park,

Ill., urges people to learn the details of their insurance policies and to keep careful records of all contacts with their insurance provider. Other recommendations: Patients should ask their doctors for letters of support stating why a specific course of treatment is necessary and stressing the medical repercussions of the illness, and mail these to their employer and the medical director of their insurance company.

While accurate data are hard to come by, experts estimate about 11 million people in the U.S.—90 percent of whom are female—suffer from either anorexia or bulimia, and many millions more may suffer from binge-eating disorder. Females with anorexia are 12 times more likely to die than other women their age in the general population. The most common causes of death are suicide or physical complications of the disorder, such as cardiac arrest resulting from electrolyte imbalances.

[T]here are no drugs approved to treat eating disorders, so a successful course of treatment is often individualized and hard to predict.

Expensive Treatment, Sometimes for Decades

Many patients don't need hospitalization and can deal with their issues with a therapist or in outpatient treatment, but those who do need inpatient care may require three to nine months or more in an eating-disorder unit of a hospital or a private treatment facility. Typically, this type of treatment can cost between $1,000 and $1,500 a day. Visits with therapists and nutritionists, plus medicine for anxiety or depression, can add tens of thousands of dollars to the total bill. Experts say only about half of the patients diagnosed with anorexia or bulimia fully recover, and the earlier the diagnosis the better the chances. Many people struggle with these diseases for decades, even some who have undergone treatment.

Insurance coverage of the disorders isn't standardized and depends largely on both the insurance carrier and the health-care plan an employer purchases. When a patient is so sick she needs to be hospitalized to stabilize organ functions, the care usually is covered as a biological illness. But once doctors determine that a patient's physical health is steady—often when she reaches a certain percentage of her ideal body weight, such as 85 percent—the disorder then is classified by the insurance company as a mental illness. At this point, though, the underlying cause of the illness may not have been addressed.

Most insurance plans place tighter limits on mental-health benefits, typically allowing for between 30 days (for an HMO [health maintenance organization]) and 60 days (for a PPO [preferred provider organization]) of psychiatric inpatient hospitalization per year. Some insurers cover less. About 40 states have so-called mental-health-parity laws, which prohibit insurers from discriminating between mental and physical illnesses. Many require insurance carriers to cover treatment for mental and emotional disorders that are biologically based, such as depression or bipolar disorder. Yet only about a dozen of these laws specifically include eating disorders.

Another problem: Unlike for many mental illnesses, there are no drugs approved to treat eating disorders, so a successful course of treatment is often individualized and hard to predict. Insurers say they follow the American Psychiatric Association's guidelines for treatment of eating disorders, but that they are reluctant to pay for extended treatment because there is no research that shows that longer treatment produces better results. "In today's environment, the real question has to be: What does the evidence show?" says Susan Pisano, spokeswoman for the Health Insurance Association of America, an industry group.

When insurance runs out, the expense can be devastating. To pay for his daughter's care, Mr. Hall says he has charged about $30,000 on credit cards and cashed in an additional $25,000 in stocks and bonds. He has used up the $100,000 in his children's college funds and sold everything he could: his home in Chicago, a second home in Michigan, a commercial building he owned and assorted extras, including a speed boat, several jet skis and an antique Corvette. "I liquidated everything." But, he says, it wasn't enough: Creditors call every day.

A Bill of Rights for People with Eating Disorders

Parents are pushing back. In New Jersey, several families of patients with eating disorders recently sued insurance companies, including Horizon Blue Cross Blue Shield of New Jersey and Aetna. Each lawsuit seeks class-action status, alleging the insurers curtailed coverage of patients' eating disorder treatment because they classified the diseases as nonbiological.

Horizon Blue Cross Blue Shield of New Jersey confirmed it is being sued but said it doesn't comment on pending litigation. Aetna didn't respond to requests for comment.

Advocacy efforts also appear to be gaining momentum. This fall, the Academy for Eating Disorders, or AED, an international association of professionals working in the field, published the Worldwide Charter for Action on Eating Disorders, a bill of rights for people with eating disorders and their families. The document calls for insurance companies and health-care systems to provide coverage for the disorders that is equal to the treatment available to people with any major illness.

The academy is working with other organizations in the field, including the National Eating Disorders Association, or NEDA, and some insurance companies to create a process to accredit treatment facilities and individuals. "The idea behind it is that if we as professionals can set standards to begin with, we can persuade the insurance companies to support those criteria and to link those to reimbursement," says Eric van Furth, president of AED. The accreditation is expected to begin next year.

NEDA recently launched a program called States for Treatment Access and Research, or STAR, to inform people about how they can push for state mental-health-parity legislation. And in New Jersey, a group of parents created an organization to support a pending state bill that would require insurance companies to treat mental illnesses that have no biological basis as they would any other illness. (Current New Jersey law requires parity in coverage only for mental illnesses that have a biological component.) The parents have met with state senators and the governor's health policy adviser and have formed a Web site to encourage others to get involved.

For Mr. Hall, the battle has become nearly too much to bear. Although he switched insurance providers this fall, his daughter, Meghan, has already reached her coverage limit and he says he has run out of money to pay for treatment privately. Meghan, who is scheduled to graduate from college . . . [within days], was admitted last week to a public psychiatric hospital in suburban Chicago. But the facility lacks a specialized eating-disorder program. "I have never felt so drained and whipped," Mr. Hall says. "Our health-care system has broken me down to nothingness in the past 2 1/2 years."

Organizations to Contact

The editors have compiled the following list of organizations concerned with the issues debated in this book. The descriptions are derived from materials provided by the organizations. All have publications or information available for interested readers. The list was compiled on the date of publication of the present volume; the information provided here may change. Be aware that many organizations take several weeks or longer to respond to inquiries, so allow as much time as possible.

Academy for Eating Disorders
60 Revere Dr., Suite 500, Northbrook, IL   60062-1577
(847) 498-4274 • fax: (847) 480-9282
e-mail: info@aedweb.org
Web site: www.aedweb.org

The Academy for Eating Disorders (AED) is an international professional organization that promotes research, treatment, and prevention of eating disorders. The AED provides education, training, and a forum for collaboration and professional dialogue.

Alliance for Eating Disorders Awareness
PO Box 13155, North Palm Beach, FL   33408-3155
(561) 841-0900 • fax: (561) 841-0972
Web site: www.eatingdisorderinfo.org

The goal of the Alliance for Eating Disorders Awareness is to establish national programs that allow children and young adults the opportunity to learn about eating disorders and the positive effects of a healthy body image. The Alliance disseminates educational information to parents and caregivers about the warning signs, dangers, and consequences of anorexia, bulimia, and other related disorders.

Eating Disorders Anonymous
P.O. Box 55876, Phoenix, AZ 85078
e-mail: info@eatingdisordersanonymous.org
Web site: www.eatingdisordersanonymous.org

Eating Disorders Anonymous (EDA) is a fellowship of individuals who share their experiences, strengths, and hopes with each other with the goal of solving their common problems and helping others to recover from their eating disorders. Members of EDA identify and claim milestones of recovery. The only requirement for membership is a desire to recover from an eating disorder. There are no dues or fees for EDA membership.

Eating Disorders Coalition
611 Pennsylvania Ave. SE, Washington, DC 20003-4303
(202) 543-9570
Web site: www.eatingdisorderscoalition.org

The Eating Disorders Coalition for Research, Policy & Action (EDC) is a cooperative of professional and advocacy-based organizations committed to federal advocacy on behalf of people with eating disorders, their families, and professionals working with these populations. The mission of the EDC is to advance the federal recognition of eating disorders as a public health priority.

Eating Disorder Foundation
3003 E. Third Ave., Suite 110, Denver, CO 80206
(303) 322-3373
Web site: www.eatingdisorderfoundation.org

The Eating Disorder Foundation is a not-for-profit organization whose mission is to be an effective resource to the general public and the health-care community in the collective effort to prevent and eliminate eating disorders. The foundation engages in education and advocacy initiatives together with timely support and help in identifying appropriate treatment options for individuals with eating disorders and their families.

Eating Disorder Referral and Information Center
2923 Sandy Pointe, Suite 6, Del Mar, CA   92014-2052
(858) 792-7463 • fax: (775) 261-9364
e-mail: edreferral@aol.com
Web site: www.edreferral.com

Eating Disorder Referral and Information Center (EDRIC) provides resources for all forms of eating disorders. EDRIC's goal is to provide assistance to those suffering from eating disorders in order to help them start on the road to recovery and healthy living.

National Eating Disorders Association
603 Steward St., Suite 803, Seattle, WA   98101
(206) 382-3587
E-mail: info@NationalEatingDisorders.org
Web site: www.nationaleatingdisorders.org

The National Eating Disorders Association (NEDA) works to prevent eating disorders and provides treatment referrals to those suffering from anorexia, bulimia, and binge eating, as well as those concerned with body image and weight issues. NEDA develops prevention programs for a wide range of audiences, publishes and distributes educational materials, and operates a toll-free eating disorders information and referral helpline.

Bibliography

Books

Cynthia Bulik and Nadine Taylor *Runaway Eating: The 8-Point Plan to Conquer Adult Food and Weight Obsessions.* Emmaus, PA: Rodale, 2005.

Simona Giordano *Understanding Eating Disorders: Conceptual and Ethical Issues in the Treatment of Anorexia and Bulimia Nervosa.* New York: Oxford University Press, 2005.

Lindsey Hall and Leigh Cohn *Bulimia: A Guide to Recovery.* Carlsbad, CA: Gürze, 1999.

Sharlene Hesse-Biber *The Cult of Thinness.* New York: Oxford University Press, 2007.

Marya Hornbacher *Wasted: A Memoir of Anorexia and Bulimia.* New York: HarperCollins, 1998.

Karen Koenig *The Food and Feelings Workbook: A Full Course Meal on Emotional Health.* Carlsbad, CA: Gürze, 2007.

John L. Levitt *Self-Harm Behaviors and Eating Disorders.* New York: Brunner-Routledge, 2004.

Aimee Liu *Gaining: The Truth About Life After Eating Disorders.* New York: Warner, 2007.

James Lock and Daniel Le Grange *Help Your Teenager Beat an Eating Disorder.* New York: Guilford, 2005.

Margo Maine and Joe Kelly *The Body Myth: Adult Women and the Pressure to Be Perfect.* Hoboken, NJ: John Wiley & Sons, 2005.

Richard Maisel, David Epston, and Ali Borden *Biting the Hand that Starves You: Inspiring Resistance to Anorexia/ Bulimia.* New York: W.W. Norton, 2004.

Randi McCabe, Traci McFarlane, and Marion Olmstead *The Overcoming Bulimia Workbook: Your Comprehensive, Step-By-Step Guide to Recovery.* Oakland: New Harbinger, 2004.

Deborah Marcontell Michel and Susan G. Willard *When Dieting Becomes Dangerous: A Guide to Understanding and Treating Anorexia and Bulimia.* New Haven: Yale University, 2003.

Dianne Neumark-Sztainer *I'm, Like, SO Fat!: Helping Your Teen Make Healthy Choices About Eating and Exercise in a Weight-Obsessed World.* New York: Guilford Press, 2005.

Sheila M. Reindl *Sensing the Self: Women's Recovery from Bulimia.* Cambridge, MA: Harvard University Press, 2001.

Grainne Smith *Anorexia and Bulimia in the Family: One Parent's Practical Guide to Recovery.* Hoboken, NJ: John Wiley & Sons, 2004.

Periodicals

Nicholas Bakalar	"Survey Puts New Focus on Binge Eating as a Diagnosis," *New York Times*, February 13, 2007.
Elizabeth Bernstein	"Men, Boys Lack Options to Treat Eating Disorders," *Wall Street Journal*, April 17, 2007.
B. Bower	"Starved for Assistance: Coercion Finds a Place in the Treatment of Two Eating Disorders," *Science News*, January 20, 2007.
Jeff Evans	"Factors Driving Anorexia, Bulimia Are Complex," *Clinical Psychiatry News*, December 2006.
Sandra G. Goodman	"Eating Disorders: Not Just for Women; Study Finds Men Are Also Prone to Risky Food Habits," *Washington Post*, March 13, 2007.
Katherine Halmi	"A Complicated Process: Diagnosing Anorexia Nervosa and Bulimia Nervosa," *Psychiatric Times*, May 1, 2005.
Nanci Hellmich	"Athletes' Hunger to Win Fuels Eating Disorders," *USA Today*, February 5, 2006.
Sarah Pressman Lovinger	"Interpersonal Therapy Aids Obese Binge Eaters," *Family Practice News*, February 15, 2007.
Diana Mahoney	"Obsessions and Compulsions Continue After Bulimia Remits," *Clinical Psychiatry News*, August 2006.

Marie McCullough — "Eating Disorders Hit Older Women; More Seek Help with Bulimia in Middle Age," *Chicago Tribune*, October 11, 2006.

Eric Nagourney — "Web Sites Celebrate a Deadly Thinness," *New York Times*, June 7, 2005.

Sarina Rosenberg — "Addicted to Exercise," *Newsweek*, April 23, 2007.

Karen Springen — "Health: Battle of the Binge," *Newsweek*, February 19, 2007.

Sally Wadyka — "Weighing In: The Latest Debate Over Models and Measurements Raises the Question, What Is Beauty?" *Vogue*, December 2006.

Womens's Health News — "Eating Disorders: A Midlife Crisis for Some Women," March 18, 2007. www.womenshealth.gov.

Index

A

Akathisia, 74
American Journal of Psychiatry, 76
Anorexia
  fatalities from, 65
  imitative, 23
  older women do not show
    classic symptoms of, 57
  prevalence in female college
    students, 29
  prevalence of, in women vs.
    men, 22
  self-starvation in, 20, 30
  web sites promoting, 60,
    64–65
Applegate, Elizabeth, 53

B

Baum, Antonia, 53
*The Beginner's Guide to Eating
Disorder Recovery* (Kolodny),
30–31
Behavior therapy, is more effective
than hospitalization in treating
bulimia, 78–81
Berman, Jenn, 61, 64, 65
Bingeing
  health effects of, 14
  sedative effect of, 18–19
Body image
  cultural impacts on, 9, 22–24,
    66
  disorders of, 23–24
  impact of college life on,
    29–30
  obsession with, as characteris-
    tic of eating disorders, 19
Body Wars (Maine), 64

Bulimia/bulimics
  antidepressants are highly suc-
    cessful in treatment of,
    70–74
  are driven by idea of good
    body, 21–32
  athletics can contribute to,
    51–54
  behavior therapy is more ef-
    fective than hospitalization
    in treating, 78–81
  characteristics of, 11, 18,
    79–80
  connection between shame
    and, 33–42
  as form of self-injury, 43–50
  many appear healthy, 16–20
  medical problems associated
    with, 13–15
  older women do not show
    classic symptoms of, 57
  secret nature of, 12–13
  symptom management as goal
    of therapy for, 71–72

C

Chernin, Kim, 22
Clinical Journal of Sport Medicine,
52
Cognitive behavior therapy, 72
Colleges, prevalence of eating dis-
  orders on, 29–32

D

Depression, associated with bulimia, 12, 23

E

Eating behaviors, Internet often
  shapes, 59–69